Better Practice
Better Golf

Better Practice Better Golf

*The Ultimate Guide to Golf Practice and
Playing Your Best Golf on the Course*

Dr. Nicky Lumb PhD

Dr. Dave Alred MBE PhD

Better Practice Better Golf

betterpracticebettergolf.com

First published in Great Britain in 2020 by Blue Horizon Publishing, a division of Blue Horizon Digital Solutions Ltd - bluehorizondigital.co.uk

ISBN 978-0-9955738-4-0

A CIP catalogue record for this book is available from the British Library.

10 9 8 7 6 5 4 3 2 1

No responsibility or liability is held for any loss or injury sustained from using the information within this book. If you have any doubts about your physical health, consult a medical professional before beginning any training programme.

Contents

INTRODUCTION

A single golf shot can be the difference between realising or not fulfilling a lifelong dream. In a 36-hole or 72-hole championship, that's less than 1% of a player's final score. Whether you hope to win a monthly medal, secure a tour card, or triumph in a major championship, you must try to make every shot count.

Golf is one of the few sports where we usually practice in a different environment than where we play (golf range vs. golf course). On the golf course, we play a different shot every time. On the driving range, we typically practice the same shot again and again. This can often lead to frustration when our improvement in practice does not transfer directly onto the course. Rather than focus on performing perfectly in practice, we should seek to play better.

The purpose of this book is to help you play better golf by improving the effectiveness and efficiency of your practice. Time is scarce for everyone, so we must make every moment of practice count, just as each shot on the golf course counts. This book will encourage you to spend time practicing the shots that will lower your scores the most, and help you to more effectively transfer your skills onto the course and into competition. Through practice, you can turn four shots into three, and three shots into two, so that it's your final score that is one shot less than everyone else's.

PART I - HOW TO PRACTICE

PRACTICE

The purpose of practice is to develop your skills so you can execute them effectively when you are playing and competing. There are three main categories of practice: technical, training and tournament. While distinct in their purpose, at times they overlap to form a continuum of practice. Spending time within each of these crucial areas will help you to play better golf.

Categories of Practice

Technical

Technical practice involves developing your technique and working on parts of your set-up or swing you want to improve. This usually involves trying to move in new ways that often feel awkward and uncomfortable at first. To get the most benefit from your technical practice, start by focusing on making a movement rather than worrying about where the ball goes. Be willing to make mistakes, so you can learn from them, as you practice each new move. Through repetition and perseverance, you will progress from getting the odd swing right in a jerky and hesitant manner to getting a few correct. The more you do it, the easier your swing will feel and as you continue to practice, you will hone your new skill until it becomes automatic and effortless.

While good technique can help you to play better golf, it does not prepare you for competitive golf. Technical practice often focuses on hitting one shot after another with the same club, whereas playing on the golf course rarely calls for the same club twice in a row. Thus, technical practice must be balanced with training and tournament practice.

Training

Training develops skills and improves ball control, preparing you to get the ball as close to the target as possible. It focuses on golf shots instead of golf swings, and is achieved by playing games with scoring systems and recording and monitoring your scores so you see your skills improve over time. Training practice can involve a lot of repetition, but it is not about repetitive repetition.

On the course, every shot is unique. You have a different lie, distance and target, so your brain has to prepare for each shot by going through a number of thought processes. In contrast, during practice, most golfers hit the same shot to the same target many times in a row. This continuous repetition makes it difficult to give each shot their full attention. To make your practice most effective, treat every shot as if it is unique so that your brain prepares to hit each ball as it would on the course. You can do this by adopting a one shot one opportunity mindset.

Dr Nicky Lumb & Dr Dave Alred MBE

This sounds straight forward but it is extremely hard to do. When we hit a number of similar shots in a row, our brains usually make assumptions about the next one based on the knowledge gained from the previous shot, instead of analysing it as if it is a completely new one. This results in less benefit and poorer concentration on each additional shot. There are counteractive strategies you can implement to make your practice more effective, and these are discussed throughout this book.

Tournament

Tournament practice attempts to replicate competitive golf, where every shot is different and you have one opportunity to execute it effectively. This practice method involves scoring every ball you hit, being accountable and getting used to performing under pressure.

Tournament practice is the ultimate test in determining whether the skills you learned or refined during technical and training practice will hold up in competition. Usually, the more often a shot matches your intention, the better your skills will transfer onto the course and into competition.

On the course, the result of your last shot informs the next one, so you do not always know which shot you will play next. It is helpful to create this element of unpredictability during tournament practice as well.

Periodisation

The time of year should influence the proportion of time you allocate to technical, training and tournament practice. During the season when you are regularly competing, it's productive to spend more time sharpening your skills (training) and replicating competitive conditions (tournament) and less time working on your swing technique, unless you need to address a specific technical issue.

Most golfers see their swings as a constant work in progress because there are always parts they want to work on and improve. Since a swing requires the precise coordination of many movements, there is a small margin for error, so any changes can be disruptive at first, with players often feeling they get worse before they get better.

For long-term improvement, it is best to plan your year by breaking it into sections and allocating specific times to focus on your playing skills and improving your swing technique. Developing your swing technique during the off-season gives you plenty of time to learn and ingrain new movements and build confidence in them before the start of the playing season.

During the playing season when you are focusing on training and tournament practices, try to allocate a few minutes of technical practice to each session. This will enable you to check your basic fundamentals including grip, ball position, posture and alignment. It is also

Dr Nicky Lumb & Dr Dave Alred MBE

productive to reinforce good swing movements so that you reduce the likelihood of developing bad habits.

As a general guide during the season, aim to spend about 20% of your practice time on your technical training, and 80% on training and tournament practices. In the off-season, if you are making a swing change, you may initially spend 80% of your practice time on technical practice and 20% between the other two areas. After a few weeks, gradually introduce more training and then tournament practice.

Technical, Training and Tournament Practice Proportion Guide

In Season (no serious technical issue)

20% Technical, 40% Training, 40% Tournament

In Season (serious technical issue)

50% Technical, 25% Training, 25% Tournament
(Do this for as short a time as possible and then revert to the usual in season guide.)

Off-Season (no swing change)

20% Technical, 40% Training, 40% Tournament

Off-Season (making a swing change)

80% Technical, 10% Training, 10% Tournament
(First couple of weeks)
60% Technical, 30% Training, 10% Tournament

40% Technical, 40% Training, 20% Tournament

30% Technical, 40% Training, 30% Tournament

20% Technical, 40% Training, 40% Tournament

Types of Practice

Within technical, training and tournament practice, there are a variety of practice options. Each one has its benefits, so it's important to always choose the most appropriate one for your requirements.

Blocked Practice

Blocked practice involves hitting a ball to the same target with the same club from the same place over and over again. Traditionally, this is how most golfers practice.

The repetition can help you to learn a skill, but be cautious how often you use it as there are few similarities between the predictability of blocked practice and the unpredictability of the next shot when you are playing golf. When you can execute a new movement with some reliability and confidence, start to incorporate more challenging types of practice that better emulate playing golf, i.e. hitting shots to different targets.

Warning!

The repetitive nature of blocked practice can lead to the temptation to hit balls quickly without giving proper thought to each shot. To combat this, take the time to thoroughly think through every shot so that you get maximum benefit. Keeping your supply of balls away from your hitting area or cleaning your club face with a towel after each shot can help you to do this by giving you a mental break between shots.

Variable Practice

Variable practice involves hitting shots in different ways so that you become more adaptable and better at contrasting between different feels. For example, using the same club to hit the ball different distances, e.g. 20, 40, 60 and 80 yards.

When you are working on your swing technique, variable practice can sometimes mean trying to do the exact opposite to what you usually do. This can help you feel the contrast between two extremes, making it easier to find a happy medium. If you hit most shots towards the heel of the club face, then learning to hit the ball off the toe can help you find the middle. Similarly, if you naturally hit a draw that sometimes turns into an uncontrollable hook, then learning the contrasting feel required to hit a fade can make it easier to neutralise shot shapes and give you a better chance of correcting it. Sometimes mixing up what you would usually associate as good or bad can help you to develop better awareness because it pushes you beyond the correction point so that the actual correction feels more achievable and comfortable.

Serial Practice

Serial practice is a form of variable practice and involves practicing in a sequence. Hitting to targets at 10, 20, 30 and 40 yards, and then repeating the sequence, forces you to think about what you are going to do for every shot, as you cannot repeat the previous movement. This strengthens

Dr Nicky Lumb & Dr Dave Alred MBE

and develops your critical thinking as well as your ability to switch between shots, and it is a step closer to playing golf compared to blocked practice which involves hitting the same shot to the same target repeatedly.

Random Practice

Random practice is playing a different shot every time. It is the closest form of practice to playing golf. Once you can successfully execute a skill, random practice is one of the fastest ways to improve, as it makes your brain constantly recall how to play different shots, which further strengthens its neural patterns. For random practice to be most effective, it should be unpredictable, so you should not know which shot you are going to play next.

The Practice Paradox

During practice, golfers often feel their skills have risen to a new level. They strike the ball better, hit more accurate shots and hole more putts, but when they go onto the course, they see little or no improvement. This is because the way they practiced had little or no resemblance to playing golf. Performance in practice does not always indicate how much is being learned. On the driving range, we often use the same club and hit to the same target from the same place many times, and this repetition makes it easier to hit more accurate shots. On the course, we only hit the same shot twice if the first one goes out of bounds. On the driving range, we can repeatedly hit balls whilst putting little or no thought into it. On the course, we have to make decisions before every shot.

Practice should be an extension of what you do on the course. When you hit the same shot time and time again, you can unconsciously switch to autopilot. By instead changing clubs, targets and distances after each shot, you may not get the immediate success that repetitive blocked practice produces, but your long-term learning and performance gains on the course will be much greater because you will be practicing playing golf.

Learning vs. Performance

In one of my PhD studies, I explored how practice influences learning and performance by investigating the differences in shot accuracy between players who engaged in just blocked practice and those who combined blocked, serial and random practice on shots between 50 and 100 yards over 10 practice sessions.

The results showed that players who only used blocked practice were more accurate in the practice sessions, but the players who engaged in blocked, serial and random practice were learning and benefiting more. This demonstrates that the benefits of practice are not always immediately evident. Instead, they are often seen days or weeks later because the brain needs time to process and consolidate what it has learned.

You will benefit most when you mentally apply yourself to each shot, so do your best to give every shot your

Dr Nicky Lumb & Dr Dave Alred MBE

full attention. It is important to know that your immediate performance in practice is not necessarily indicative of how much you are learning. When you mentally commit to executing a shot and don't succeed, your brain still learns. Signs of improvement usually take time and more time than we think it should!

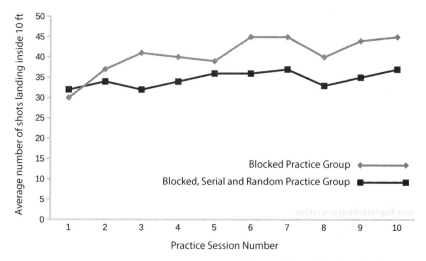

Figure 1. Practice Session Results

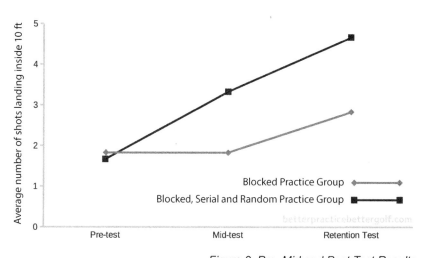

Figure 2. Pre, Mid and Post Test Results

Designing Practice

How you practice can have a huge impact on how you learn, play and perform. One of the keys to effective practice is making it measurable so you can monitor your progress over time. This can be done by setting target scores to achieve in the fewest shots possible or by adding pressure with a consequence, for example, starting again if a target score is not met.

It is more preferable to set a target score and to keep going until you achieve it than it is to hit a certain number of shots. For putts between 3ft and 10ft, instead of seeing how many putts out of ten you can hole, set a target of holing 10 putts and record how many attempts it takes to achieve. Knowing you have to hole 10 putts to complete the practice increases concentration and incentivises you to learn from each one.

Holing 10 putts is also more beneficial psychologically, because when you finish the practice, you will have achieved the positive goal of holing ten putts. If you instead attempted 10 putts, holed 4 and missed 6, then it could be demoralising to know you missed more than you holed, and if you holed seven but missed three, your brain could still interpret it negatively.

You can take this formula further by introducing pressure through setting the same goal with the caveat that if you miss a putt, you have to start again from the beginning or deduct a certain number of putts that you have already holed. This builds resilience and toughness. Many golfers

Dr Nicky Lumb & Dr Dave Alred MBE

will give up after a few attempts if they haven't managed to complete the practice, whereas those most determined will keep going until they succeed. This often creates a mental attitude which helps players to cope better with shots that don't match their intention in competition.

Challenge

If a practice is too easy, there will be little or no learning and you are likely to get bored. If a practice is too hard, learning slows down and you will experience minimal success which can affect your confidence and enjoyment. This creates a fine line between developing your skills and growing your confidence.

One of the keys to effective practice is finding a balance between making your practice sufficiently challenging while at the same time enabling you to achieve some success. In general, the more challenging a practice is, the more you will learn, but the less successful your performance is likely to be.

For your practice to be most effective, you should constantly push yourself to the edge or just beyond your current ability, so you are always practicing at your margin. If it takes you 20 putts to hole 12 putts between 3ft and 5ft, you should aim to complete the practice in 19 attempts. When this is achieved, aim to do it in 18 putts and always note your scores so that you know what your performance targets are. If you are practicing lag putting and can consistently get putts inside 20ft within two feet of the hole but struggle around 24ft, start your sessions at 20ft and work back from there, so you are always challenging yourself.

By recording and monitoring your practice results, you can determine if your practices are set at the most appropriate level. In scoring games, a success rate between 60% and 70% is a good guide. If your scoring percentages are higher, make the practices harder. If your scores are much lower, make them easier. Most golfers stop improving because they do not push themselves when they practice, so make your practice challenging—ideally more so than competing on the course. If it doesn't challenge you, it will not improve you!

Consequences

On the course, there is a consequence to every shot. If you have a favourable or fair outcome, you are likely to be happy or impassive. If a ball does not finish where you want it to, then at times you will probably be irritated. How often do you experience these feelings in practice? Ideally the consequences in practice should be worse and more penalizing than those experienced in a competition, yet most golfers practice in a relaxed state, which makes them ill-prepared for the pressures they will face.

Creating pressure by practicing with consequences will change the physical wiring of your brain and make you more resilient in high-stakes situations. You can do this by making yourself accountable and scoring the process and/ or the outcome of every shot. For example, you may set a target of getting up and down three times, and you cannot

Dr Nicky Lumb & Dr Dave Alred MBE

finish until this is achieved. Or you can make it tougher by having to achieve three consecutive up and downs, with the penalty consequence of starting over if you miss one. If you have got up and down twice and only need one more, but missing the next one means starting again, your heart tends to beat much faster!

Playing against others for money can also create pressure outside of official competitions. Other options include having to do press-ups, depriving yourself of your favourite dessert or choosing an unwelcome penalty if you miss shots or don't reach target scores.

A good way to start every practice session is making yourself hole five different five-foot putts either in isolation or in a row. This instils a good mindset for the session and immediately introduces pressure. When you have planned a session and have to achieve this just to get off first base, you'll be surprised how much pressure you feel.

Quantity vs. Quality

Hitting lots of balls and accruing numerous hours on the practice ground builds confidence for some players. However, one of the keys to effective practice is not just how much you do but what you do. Don't fall into the trap of mistaking quantity for quality. Giving every shot a purpose and changing clubs and targets after each ball will be of more benefit than rapidly firing twice as many balls with one or two clubs to a single target.

Playing golf is ultimately 'one shot one opportunity.' On the course your next shot is always different to the previous one. This makes the number of 'first shots' you have in practice crucial in determining how relevant your practice will be towards improving on the course. Your practice should be an extension of what you do on the course, and you should be able to play well on the course by doing exactly what you do in practice. Quality will always beat quantity.

Number of Balls Per Set

You need to be alert and consciously aware of what you are trying to do to get the most benefit from each shot. To maximize your concentration, hit balls in sets of no more than five. If you feel five is too many, drop it to two or three. This will create some repetition but it provides a good number of 'first' shots, and more closely replicates playing golf. Keep your supply of balls away from the hitting zone so you have to go and collect your next set. This will give you a mental break and encourage your brain to fully prepare for the next shot.

Number of Shots Per Practice

The number of shots hit in each practice will vary, but as a general guide, aim to hit a maximum of 50 shots before moving on to something else. There's nothing wrong with going back to a practice later in a session to finish it, and to get the most benefit, you must be alert. Another alternative is to run two or three practices at the same time alongside

Dr Nicky Lumb & Dr Dave Alred MBE

each other, so you hit one wedge shot or a set of wedges, followed by a drive or a set of drives and then go back to the wedge practice and repeat the cycle. This variation will help to keep you more alert, more closely represents how you play on the course, and will improve your level of learning as it gives you more 'first' shots so you will have to think through each shot rather than simply repeat or slightly adjust what you did on the previous one.

Score Every Practice

Golfers often evaluate their practice success by judging whether a session was good or bad, but our feelings and emotions can vary every day which gives our thoughts and evaluations little consistency. If you think you had a good practice session, then you may be more confident and upbeat, but if you feel the session went badly, you may be down and dejected. By evaluating sessions through scores, your assessments will be objective and consistent. If your goal is to get up and down nine times then either you achieve it or you don't, there is no middle ground.

It's important to know that when you mentally commit to a shot but it does not match your intention, *your brain still learns!* This is why you will often repeatedly try to play a shot and struggle, and then suddenly for no apparent reason you will succeed. Imagine your brain is collecting data and when it has stored enough, you will be able to execute the shot. The frustration is that you never know how much input it needs, so just keep going on a little and often basis until you succeed.

On the course, every shot matters, so there is a consequence for each shot. For your training and tournament practice to be most effective, try to create a consequence for every shot as well. If you practice in a relaxed state where the result of a shot doesn't matter, how can you expect to play at your best when it really does matter? When you play, you will be in the rough, have shots from awkward lies, miss greens and have to battle to save par or worse. Ideally you want to make your practice so challenging that these situations on the course feel easier.

With golf being an individual sport, it is easy to analyse your game, determine your current skill levels and set your own goals to improve. By scoring and recording every practice, you can try to beat previous scores and aim to set personal bests every time you practice. Trying to achieve a score with every shot gives each one a purpose and places a realistic pressure on you to perform. You can score a shot in terms of how well you followed one of your routines or a process within it; the quality of a strike; whether it matched your intention; or its accuracy in terms of distance, direction or both. Always record and monitor your scores so that you know how you performed. Over time, you will hopefully see your scores progress.

When you are working on your swing technique, it can sometimes be difficult to quantify progress. To overcome this, try to score the feel of what you are working on out of 10 for each shot. If you have a video camera, launch monitor or other feedback tool, give yourself a 'feel' score first. Then use the feedback tool to determine how successfully you executed the intended movement, and how accurate your feel was. This process can accelerate your progress as you can calibrate what you are feeling with what you are doing. By scoring each shot, you can calculate an average score for each session, and recording this number allows you to compare results over time.

Notebook

A notebook is an invaluable tool in helping you to improve. It will be of most benefit if you always have it with you when you play and practice, so you can write down any thoughts, swing or body feels that arise. We naturally forget approximately 70% of what we do, so it's helpful to have a resource to refer back to. Recording everything you do—including your training and tournament practice results—will make you more accountable for your actions, help you to monitor your scores over time and highlight any trends or behaviours that work well and lead to you being more effective.

It can be helpful to write on the back page of your notebook the distances you hit each club, your swing keys and favourite affirmations, so that you always have a quick reference for when you are trying to decide which club to use on the course or feel you need a prompt to help you to refocus and reset.

Little and Often

Practicing on a little and often basis is the fastest way to improve. When you learn to make a new movement or start to play a new shot, your brain creates new neural network patterns. The more often you practice, the more your brain has to recall and apply the new pattern and the stronger it becomes. Even if you are struggling to master the technique, the thought process of trying to execute the skill will still be strengthening the patterns in your brain. With ever increasing repetitions, these patterns become more established until your brain is able to relegate what was once a new movement to its subconscious, and you will be able to do it automatically most of the time.

Mix It Up

A few years ago, I coached some of Malaysia's top amateur golfers at TPC Kuala Lumpur on the LPGA Development Programme. On the first day, I set up some chipping and putting practices on the main practice green, and I was amazed how good the players' scores were. The following day, I repeated the practices on the course and used greens which the players were unfamiliar with. Their scores dropped by almost 50%, and the practices took much longer. I didn't expect it to affect their scores so much, and the experience taught me an invaluable lesson in effective practice design.

Some courses are very tight and have lots of surrounding water, gorse bushes and out of bounds, whilst others are wide open with little trouble in sight. Broaden your golf experiences and play different courses so you get used to various conditions. A dry links or heathland course will play very differently to a wet American-style course, and varying grass textures will challenge your ball striking. Just as the familiarity of hitting balls on the driving range with the same club to the same target can encourage mindless hitting, so can playing the same course. Counteract this by expanding your playing experiences on different courses as often as possible.

When you practice your short game, use different greens and continually change holes, so you always have to make new reads and choose new landing spots. If you become familiar with a green's breaks and undulations, there can be a temptation to be less attentive in your decision-making which will affect the efficacy of your practice. Remember golf is 'one shot one opportunity.'

It is also productive to play with different people on a regular basis, as this reduces the familiarity you get from playing with the same people and will help you to improve. You may feel uncomfortable doing this at first, but it will benefit your golf!

Competition

The more fun you have when you practice, the more motivated you will be to do it. The more you practice, the better golfer you will become. Turning much of your practice into a competition and playing games against yourself or others should increase your enjoyment especially if you record and monitor your scores, as every practice session will give you an opportunity to beat your previous scores and achieve a new personal best.

Shot Making

On the course, every shot is different, and it isn't possible to have previously practiced every shot you will play during a round. To play any shot, you will use your own unique swing and combine it with choosing a club and determining the swing length, speed, force and power you will need to apply. You will then need to decide on your grip position, ball position and stance. The more experience you have playing different shots, the more automatic and subconscious these decisions will be, and the more capable you will be at creating shots that you have not previously played.

On the second playoff hole in the 2012 Masters at Augusta National, Bubba Watson hit his drive way right and into the trees. With 155 yards to the flag and seemingly no option other than to come out sideways, he hooked the ball over 40 yards around trees and a TV tower before landing it on the green and spinning it up the slope to around 15 feet. The shot won him his first green jacket and was a fantastic example of how many shots in golf are more of an art than a science.

To become more creative and improve your shot making skills regularly complete some of the practices with clubs you usually wouldn't use, and frequently play on the course with less than 14 clubs. Playing rounds with only your odd or even numbered clubs is beneficial and the 'Be Creative with 5-clubs' practice in the On the Course practice section is great fun and will really develop your shot making skills.

Dr Nicky Lumb & Dr Dave Alred MBE

Course vs. Range Practice

There are major differences in how golfers traditionally practice on a driving range and play on the course. If we can better replicate playing golf in practice, then we are more likely to improve our scores on the course.

Typical Driving Range Behaviours	Golf Course Behaviours	Suggested Driving Range Behaviours
Hit to the same target or no target	Hit each shot to a different target	Hit to different, small, precise targets
Use the same club for consecutive shots	Change the club after every shot	Change clubs after every shot or at least 5 shots
Pay little or no attention to a shot's distance	Hit to different distances	Hit to different distances
Hit from flat lies	Hit from different lies	Hit from flat lies (this is usually unavoidable)
Little or no intention on any shot	A clear intention on every shot	Create a clear intention on every shot
Hit balls quickly	Take up to 40 seconds to hit each shot	Take up to 40 seconds to hit each shot
No pre-shot routine	Pre-shot routine	Pre-shot routine
Stand still	Walk between shots	Move between shots. Go and get your next ball
Tinker with swing technique	Focus on hitting the target	Focus on hitting the target
No consequence for any shot	A consequence for every shot	Create a consequence for every shot. Repeat the shot if it doesn't match your intention

Figure 3. Course vs. Range Behaviours

Plan, Do, Review

Time is valuable, so make the most of it by planning your practice sessions in advance. Set up to three main goals per session, and practice the shots you need to, not just the ones you are good at and enjoy practicing. Start working on each shot category with a technical practice so you reinforce good technique, and then move on to training and tournament practices. Always score each shot and record your results for accountability, so you can compare scores and set new targets.

To maintain your mental engagement, mix up the practices so you do not spend too long on any one practice. If the facilities allow, do a putting practice followed by a long game one and then a short game practice, and then repeat the cycle. If possible, you could take this nearer to replicating playing golf by working on two or three practices at once and doing one putt or one set of putts followed by a full shot or a set of full shots before looping back to the putting green. We tend to remember more about the beginning and end of a session than the middle part, so it's beneficial to keep practices short and sharp.

Post-Practice Review

Reviewing sessions will help you to learn and improve. After every session list:

- What went well
- Things to improve

Dr Nicky Lumb & Dr Dave Alred MBE

- If you could rerun the practice what you would do differently
- What you can do to be better next time

What should you practice?

Playing Statistics

Our personal judgements and perceptions are subjective and not always accurate. At the end of the 2012 season, Sean Foley asked Justin Rose which areas of his game he most wanted to improve during his off-season. Justin said his wedge play, as he felt his playing partners were often more accurate with their wedges. Ironically, on the PGA Tour that year, Justin Rose had been the best player.

Playing statistics can complement your thoughts and opinions with factual evidence, identifying your strengths and weaknesses and pinpointing the shots you play the most and the least. This can help you to plan your practice and optimise your time. It will be less effective spending most of your time practicing bunker shots that represent less than 3% of your score, if driving is your weakest shot and represents 28% of your game.

By analysing thousands of shots by amateur and professional golfers, Professor Mark Broadie, author of Every Shot Counts, one of the most informative books on golf, explains the following points about how scores are formed:

The Long Game Rules

Shots over 100 yards influence scores two thirds more than shots inside 100 yards. Players who achieve lower scores hit fewer penalising shots, strike the ball better, hit more greens and land their approach shots closer to the hole.

Approach Shots

Approach shots into the green are the most important shots in golf. Iron shot accuracy accounts for 40% of the difference in standards of golfers. Hitting more greens equals lower scores, and the closer you hit your ball to the hole, the better. In his prime, Tiger Woods gained 46% of his scoring advantage with his approach shot accuracy. Between 150 and 200 yards, Tiger hit his approach shots 4 to 5 feet closer to the hole than tour average, which increased his chances of holing his first putt as well as making three putts less likely.

Driving

Driving is the second most influential shot in golf and represents 28% of the game. We usually hit between 10 and 14 drives per round, and driving distance contributes more to lower scores than driving accuracy. As a general rule when hole design allows, hit the ball as far as you can while keeping it in play.

Short Game

The short game consists of all shots inside 100 yards that are off the green and contributes 17% to scoring. Most shots that miss the green finish within 20 yards of the hole, so green side shots inside this range are a key practice distance. Although improving your long game will reduce scores the most, it is usually the hardest area to improve and takes the most time. To reduce scores the fastest, aim to improve your short game.

Putting

Putting represents 15% of the game and is the least important shot in golf. This statistic surprised many who previously thought it was the most influential shot as the putter is the most used club. Short putts inside seven feet influence scores the most, with four feet the most important distance for amateurs and five feet the key distance for pros. Good putters differentiate themselves most between three and seven feet, so spend the highest proportion of your putting practice within this range.

On the PGA Tour, players one-putt from 20 feet fifteen percent of the time, so it is hard for better players to differentiate their skill levels on longer putts. As a guide, on putts over 20ft, aim to get the ball to finish within 10% of its starting distance, e.g. within 3ft for a 30ft putt.

Recording and Analysing Your Playing Statistics

While the statistics described present generalities for most golfers, it is essential to record your playing statistics so that you can analyse your own game. By determining the shots you play the most, as well as your strengths and weaknesses, you can work out the shots that will help you to improve your game and lower your scores the most. There are many golf statistics programmes which can help you to do this including Mark Broadie's Golf Metrics system. Decade is another, and this contains an excellent course management system. Both of these programmes include Strokes Gained, a system designed by Mark Broadie that measures every shot a player hits and compares it to an average for every standard of golfer including PGA Tour players. If a player hits a shot that is better than average, the shot will have a positive stroke gained number. If a shot is worse than average, it will have a negative stroke gained number, and an average shot will be zero, neither positive nor negative. If you prefer to analyse your playing statistics yourself, the score card and results analysis charts on pages 294 and 295 will help you.

While playing statistics will give you factual information about your game, if there are shots you feel uncomfortable or unconfident playing, make sure you practice them as well. We naturally enjoy practicing what we are good at but are not always good at practicing shots we don't like playing or feel are our weaker skills, so be sure to identify these shots and give them the appropriate attention.

LEARNING

Your Swing

There Is No Perfect Swing

If you look closely, you will notice the world's best players all have unique swings. There is not a perfect swing, yet many golfers spend hours trying to achieve it, wrongly believing a great-looking swing will create better shots. A perfect looking swing will not always create a perfect strike. A perfect strike can create a perfect shot and many techniques can achieve this, even unorthodox ones.

To play good golf, you need a swing that is functional and gets the ball where you want it to go. Don't worry how it looks, and never change it to make it look better. There is no guarantee a swing that looks good will get the ball where you want it to go more often or lead to lower scores. In fact, more careers have been ruined than made by golfers who pursued a perfect swing and ignored their ball striking. There are no awards or shot reductions for the nicest-looking swing, so only modify your technique to improve the consistency of how you deliver the club face to the ball at impact. This is the only part of a swing that really matters, so focus on how you hit the ball, and be accountable for the quality of each strike.

Dr Nicky Lumb & Dr Dave Alred MBE

Trust

When you trust your swing, you can focus on the shots you want to play without the distraction of trying to consciously control your body's or club's movements. This allows you to focus on what you are doing instead of how you are doing it, which usually results in more shots that match your intention. Practicing your routines will help you to trust your processes so that you play more shots instinctively.

Tempo / Rhythm

Tempo is the overall speed of your swing, and rhythm describes the ratio of time between your backswing and downswing. On the PGA Tour, the average time is 0.75 seconds for a backswing and 0.25 seconds for the downswing, giving a backswing to downswing time ratio of 3:1. When your tempo and rhythm are synchronized, you will hit good shots, but when your tempo and rhythm are out of sync, your shots will often be less accurate and much harder to control. This can happen when you are working on your swing technique, as your body and hands can often struggle to work together when they are trying to make new movements that often feel awkward at first.

With shorter swings, this inaccuracy is often even more pronounced. If the hands travel faster than the body, then the club head will get ahead of the body which usually results in the club face being closed (facing left with a right-handed player) at impact, which causes the ball to fly left or at least start left. A lack of synchronization can also occur when the body gets ahead of the hands. The club head then falls behind the body, and the club face does not catch up before striking the ball, resulting in an open (right-facing) club face at impact and the ball starting right of the intended target.

By focusing on one part of a swing, other swing parts can be temporarily ignored, and this can reduce club face control and lead to more wayward shots. This is why it is helpful to separate practice into the three distinct categories of technical, training and tournament, so that time is allocated to improving each specific area.

Hitting into a net can help to develop your rhythm and timing, as the net encourages you to focus on your tempo without the distraction of looking to see where the ball is going. Humming a song or using a metronome and swinging in time to the rhythm can also help synchronize your body's and club's movements.

Focus of Attention

What you are thinking about when you make a swing is known as your focus of attention. If you are thinking about your body's movement(s) such as 'flat left wrist' or 'clear the hips,' you have an internal focus of attention (it's your body). When you focus on something outside of your body you have an external focus of attention. There are two types; one that is close to you such as an item you are wearing or the club you are holding; and one that is further away such as your intended ball flight or target. Logic suggests that focusing internally on how parts of your body are moving and trying to consciously control them during a swing will reduce mistakes, but it can be detrimental, as it can disrupt your swing's usual flow, making it more error prone as you have too much detailed conscious thought.

Benefits of an External Focus of Attention

Adopting an external focus can help your body to self-organise its movements so you can swing normally. Imagine you are trying to cross a road with a car speeding towards you at over 100 mph. If you react and run, you've got a better chance of making it safely to the other side than if you start to analyse your running technique. In the 2012 Masters, Tiger Woods was struggling for form and admitted he had been "playing his swing and then trying to play the course", which meant he was "focusing on movement mechanics the whole time, and when competing this is unsuccessful." When you are playing concentrate on where you want the ball to go and how you want it to get there, so you reduce the likelihood of being distracted by your swing technique which will already be in your subconscious. When you are running across a road, you are unlikley to be interested in your foot strike and instead will be consciously concerned about avoiding the traffic.

My research with a group of European Tour players suggests when players are hitting relatively straight forward shots, they tend to focus on a swing key which usually has an internal focus and involves how they would like a certain body part to move or feel. When shots become more difficult this changes and they adopt either a target orientated external focus or combine it with how they want the shot to feel (internal focus). Interestingly, when players have to play really tough shots, they focus on their intended ball flight and target, have no technical thoughts and have an external focus of attention. You can make any shot more demanding by always choosing a small precise target, even when the flag is in the middle of a large flat green!

How to Adopt an External Focus of Attention

Historically, golfers have focused internally on how parts of their body should move. Improvements in learning and performance could be large if they instead adopt an external focus and direct their attention outside of their body towards an intended outcome or movement goal. To do this think belt buckle to the target instead of clear the hips. To add width to your backswing keep the club head away from your sweater zip instead of thinking about your

Dr Nicky Lumb & Dr Dave Alred MBE

hands and chest, so that you take your focus away from your body's internal movements.

On the course, adopt an external focus of attention by identifying a small precise target and create a clear visual picture of every shot you intend to play. Following the processes described in the pre-shot routine section will help you to do this.

Learning a New Movement

How to Accelerate Your Technical Progress

Learning a new swing movement can be difficult, and the following steps can help you to progress.

1. Aim to adopt an external focus of attention and focus on the effect of the intended movement instead of the movement itself whenever you can.

2. Break the movement into parts and practice each one in isolation, so you create a feeling or thought you can replicate before you try to recreate it within a fuller movement. Doing this in slow motion and with your eyes closed can help to create greater awareness of precisely what your movements are.

3. With body movements, place your hands across your chest and make the movement without the added distraction of your arms and hands. Be mindful that your power always initiates from your core out.

4. Add your arms and hands by imagining you are holding a club, then make the new movement.

5. Make swings with a small junior club so the club head at address is hovering a few feet above the ground.

6. Massively exaggerate the movement so you feel like a funny cartoon character or imagine you are demonstrating the movement to someone else.

7. Make swings with your eyes closed so you heighten your senses and become more aware of the positions you are in.

8. Place a tee in the ground where a ball would usually be and make the new movement while brushing the tee.

Dr Nicky Lumb & Dr Dave Alred MBE

9. Make practice swings at differing speeds. Do them as slowly as possible, 50% slower than normal and at normal speed. Slow motion swings will help you to better understand your swing and the movement you are trying to make.

10. Hit balls into a net so you can focus on your swing without the distraction of where the ball is going. Do this 50% slower than normal and then at normal speed.

11. Hit balls in sets of up to 5 balls and make a practice swing between each shot. Focus on the process and getting the movement right, not where the ball finishes, unless it's relevant to what you are working on. Score the quality of each movement out of 10.

12. Use feedback from the ball's flight to guide you into adapting your technique to achieve the intended flight.

13. Choose a target zone. In sets of up to 5 balls, score the quality of each swing out of 10. Score the accuracy of each shot. Award 1 point when the ball lands in the target zone. Change the club and target after each set.

14. Go through your pre-shot routine and change the club and target after every shot. Score the accuracy of each shot. Award 1 point when the ball lands in the target zone.

Swing Aids

Swing aids can help you to create a feel for a position or movement in your swing. Some work by restricting actions and removing mistakes, while others encourage you to make a better movement by swinging around or through objects. The latter is more preferable as it gives you feedback on the movement you are making and gives you an external focus of attention.

Many golfers fall into the trap of using a swing aid repeatedly and thinking that because they are hitting balls the 'correct way,' they will master the new movement. When they remove the aid, they are disappointed because after a few shots, they are back to square one. Using a swing aid in this way is similar to blocked practice. It is good at creating success, but it is not as constructive as it could be.

To get the most benefit from a swing aid, understand exactly what the fault is, how you make it and what you need to do differently to correct it. While you are using the aid, try to verbalise the feel it is giving you and what you feel you are doing differently. The most effective learning model is to then hit 5 shots with the training aid, remembering the detail of how the movement feels, followed by 5 shots on your own trying to recreate the same movement. As you improve, use the training aid less and less so it becomes a tool for positive reinforcement, not a device you are dependent on.

Feedback

Every time you hit a shot, there is feedback. You can see the ball's flight, where it lands and finishes, and hear the sound of the club face striking the ball. Internal feedback tells you what the movement and strike felt like. External feedback from sources such as coaches, videos, launch monitors and swing aids can give you information that improves your awareness of what you are doing. Without feedback, very little learning will occur, so it's important to get feedback from every shot.

Benefits of Feedback

In one of my PhD studies, I explored how feedback during practice influences learning and performance by using a launch monitor and telling players the carry distance of their shots.

The results showed that when players know how far they just hit a shot, their shots are more accurate during practice (Figure 4) and in post practice retention tests (Figure 5) in comparison to when players do the same practices, but can only see where their shots land. This highlights the benefits of feedback and how learning and performance can be expedited with it.

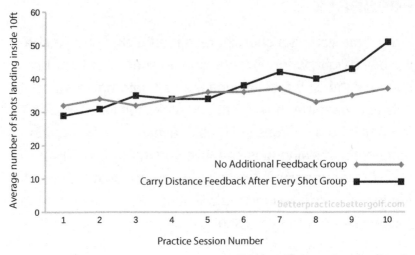

Figure 4. Practice Session Results

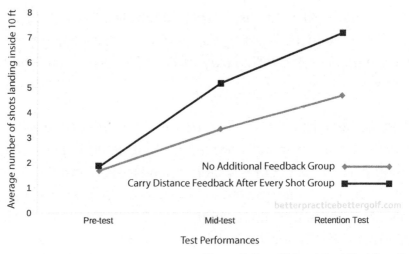

Figure 5. Pre, Mid and Post Test Results

Immediate Feedback

Immediate feedback is when you receive feedback straight after a shot. Memories and feelings fade as time passes, so

Dr Nicky Lumb & Dr Dave Alred MBE

immediate feedback is the most meaningful as it allows you to correct mistakes on the next shot based on feelings from the previous shot. There can however be a temptation to rely on it and only make error corrections, instead of trying to work out what caused the error, which is more beneficial for your long-term learning.

One way to overcome this is by predicting what you think the feedback will be before you receive it. If you are trying to strike the ball in the middle of the club face, put talc or face spray on the club face, hit your shot, predict where the club face impacted the ball, and then check the location. This will help you to build an awareness of the different feelings when you strike the ball in the centre, heel or toe. The feedback is immediate, so you should remember what the strike and swing felt like. By knowing the ball's impact location, you can adjust for the next shot to try to make it better.

If you are working on distance control and have access to a launch monitor, hit a shot and predict the carry distance before the ball lands. Then check your prediction. This will help you to calibrate your feelings and distance control. If you do not have access to a launch monitor, create target zones at specific distances on the range. Then hit a shot and immediately predict if the ball will land inside the target zone, short of it or beyond it. Check your prediction when the ball lands.

Ball Flight

The ball's flight can help you to work out the cause and effect of a shot and calibrate your internal feels. It only takes 1.5 seconds to make a swing and hit the ball. This is not enough time for anyone to see all of the intricate swing movements involved. When you hit a shot, instructors typically watch the ball's starting direction and flight and refer their observations to the ball flight laws, which help them to determine the cause and effect of the ball's behaviour. If more golfers could grasp an understanding of the ball flight laws, it would help them to detect and possibly correct their mistakes. Sometimes just a small adjustment can transform a round.

There are six factors that make up the ball flight laws: face strike, club face, club path, club speed, angle of attack and dynamic loft.

1. Face strike is where on the club face it impacts the ball. Most golfers struggle to hit the ball in the middle of the club face and instead make contact towards the heel or toe. This can adversely affect every element of a shot, and should make achieving a central strike your main priority. To achieve this, it is often helpful to try and find the middle of the club face by using half-swings at first.

2. Club face is the direction the club face is pointing in at impact. This can have up to an 80% influence on the ball's starting direction, so it's important it is pointing where you want the ball to start. If the club face is pointing at the target, the ball will start flying straight. If the club face is pointing left of the target for a right-handed player (closed), then the ball will start to fly to

the left. If it is pointing to the right (open), then the ball will start to the right.

Figure 6. Club Face Direction (for Right-handed Player)

3. Club path is the direction the club head is moving in at impact. This mainly influences the curve of the ball's flight and is the second most influential factor on the shape of a shot. There are three types of path: in to out, out to in and in to square to in. When the club face and path are pointing in the same direction, the ball will fly straight with no curve. The more disparity there is between the two, the more the ball will curve.

Figure 7. Swing Paths (for Right-handed Player)

The combinations of club face position and swing path direction create nine different ball flights: straight, slice, hook, pull, push, push slice, pull hook, draw and fade. It can be difficult to digest how all of the nine flights are created, so it is often helpful to take one constant and to then try a variation to create the intended ball flight.

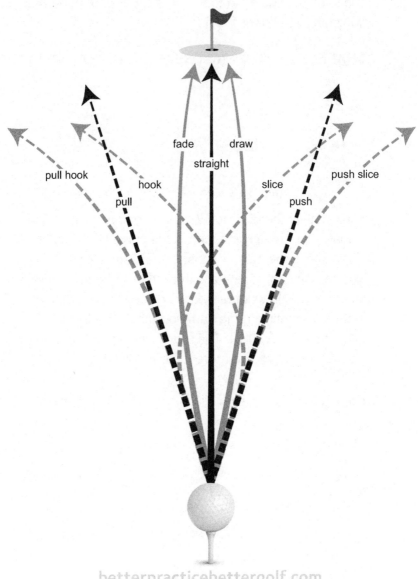

9 BALL FLIGHTS

Figure 8. 9 Ball Flights

Dr Nicky Lumb & Dr Dave Alred MBE

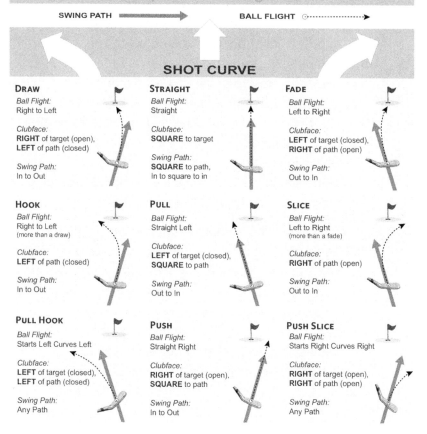

GOLF BALL FLIGHT LAWS

betterpracticebettergolf.com

SWING PATH ➡️   BALL FLIGHT ⊙·············➤

SHOT CURVE

DRAW
Ball Flight:
Right to Left

Clubface:
RIGHT of target (open),
LEFT of path (closed)

Swing Path:
In to Out

STRAIGHT
Ball Flight:
Straight

Clubface:
SQUARE to target

Swing Path:
SQUARE to path,
In to square to in

FADE
Ball Flight:
Left to Right

Clubface:
LEFT of target (closed),
RIGHT of path (open)

Swing Path:
Out to In

HOOK
Ball Flight:
Right to Left
(more than a draw)

Clubface:
LEFT of path (closed)

Swing Path:
In to Out

PULL
Ball Flight:
Straight Left

Clubface:
LEFT of target (closed),
SQUARE to path

Swing Path:
Out to In

SLICE
Ball Flight:
Left to Right
(more than a fade)

Clubface:
RIGHT of path (open)

Swing Path:
Out to In

PULL HOOK
Ball Flight:
Starts Left Curves Left

Clubface:
LEFT of target (closed),
LEFT of path (closed)

Swing Path:
Any Path

PUSH
Ball Flight:
Straight Right

Clubface:
RIGHT of target (open),
SQUARE to path

Swing Path:
In to Out

PUSH SLICE
Ball Flight:
Starts Right Curves Right

Clubface:
RIGHT of target (open),
RIGHT of path (open)

Swing Path:
Any Path

Figure 9. Ball Flight Laws (for Right-handed Player)

4. Club speed is the velocity at which the club head is travelling. The faster its speed, the greater the energy that can be transferred into the ball and the further the ball will fly. A ball will fly furthest when it is struck in the middle of the club face. For tee shots, it is important to maximize speed. On approach shots into greens, a consistent speed is needed to enhance accuracy.

5. Angle of attack is the direction the club head is travelling in through impact in terms of up or down to the ball. This influences the trajectory of a shot.

Off the tee, to maximize distance, the club face should be travelling up to the ball so a positive attack angle is achieved[1]. In contrast, to produce a solid iron strike, the lowest point of a swing should be just after the ball has been struck, so a ball followed by turf impact is achieved. By striking down and hitting the ball before the club touches the ground, all of the club's energy goes into the ball. Many golfers lose distance by hitting the ground before the ball. With a thin shot, the club face contacts the ball above its equator, so little or no grass is taken; however, the loft on the club is not fully engaged, causing a lower flight path than expected.

6. Dynamic loft is the amount of loft delivered onto the ball by the club face at impact. It is the vertical club face aim, and it influences the trajectory and distance of a shot. Too much active loft can launch the ball too high, reducing distance, while too little dynamic loft can cause a lower, shorter flight with the ball rolling more on landing. The amount of loft on a club (static loft), the strike point on the club face and angle of attack can all influence the dynamic loft.

Learn from Every Shot

To learn from every shot, try to have a clear plan for each one. This allows you to objectively evaluate if and how well a shot matched your intention, and if it did not, to try to identify why. Ask yourself, 'how does this relate to the ball flight laws and what can I do differently next time?' During practice, if you can work out an answer, act on it. If you're not sure, note the shot you were trying to play and the

---

1   Players with exceptionally fast club speeds often have to hit down on the ball off the tee to achieve better ball flight control

Dr Nicky Lumb & Dr Dave Alred MBE

ball's behaviour (i.e. where the ball started and finished in relation to the target and describe its flight) so you can work it out later. If a body part felt wrong, note it as well, so you can see if any patterns emerge over time. This information will also be useful to PGA Professionals if you decide to seek help with your game.

For example:

1. Shot – 120 yards flat lie
    Intention – Straight shot
    Result – Thin shot and the ball went straight right, body felt tense.

2. Shot – Drive
    Intention – Draw
    Result – Ball started left of target and curved right, finishing in the rough.

Sound Check

The sound of the strike can give you a good indication of where the club face struck the ball. A good strike sounds like a crisp, pure click. A heavy or fat shot is when the club head contacts the ground before the ball, and it sounds like a deep thud. A thin shot is when the club face impacts the ball above its equator, and this usually sounds tinny.

Score Your Strike

In the book The Pressure Principle, Dr Dave Alred describes a scoring system that can help you to quantify the quality of your strikes. When a strike feels perfect, give yourself zero. Use a plus number for a heavy or fat strike and a minus number when you hit a thin shot. The higher your score, the greater the mishit, and the lower the number, the better the strike, with zero being perfect and resulting in all of the energy created transferring into the ball. In comparison plus two would mean a heavy strike, some energy transferring into the ground instead of the ball, and the ball unlikely to travel its intended distance. Scoring every shot will give you a better understanding of what you are doing and what you need to do on the next shot to make it better.

Feel Isn't Real

Have you ever filmed your golf swing, watched the recording and looked twice because what you saw wasn't what you expected to see? A perplexing aspect of golf is that often what you feel and think you are doing is completely different to what you are actually doing.

I once videoed a club golfer's swing during a lesson. When we played back the recording, he was convinced it was not him, because his swing looked so different to how it felt. Only after we rerecorded his swing using his phone did he believe it was him! For this reason, video analysis can be invaluable in helping us to learn and relate to what we are actually doing, but it can take a bit of time to get used to!

Dr Nicky Lumb & Dr Dave Alred MBE

Less is More

Getting the right amount of relevant feedback is important. If you try to apply too much at once, you may struggle to keep everything in mind and thus gain little benefit.

When feedback is kept simple and concise, it is easier to understand and apply, and improvements can be made more quickly. Aim to apply feedback in small, manageable pieces by having one clear thought when you stand over the ball and possibly one other during your swing.

If you are practicing with a launch monitor, the software on most devices gives copious amounts of feedback after every shot. This information is invaluable for an overview of your swing, but once you have decided what you will work on, try to limit yourself to seeing one parameter after each shot. If you need more, use a maximum of three.

Describe the Solution

Feedback can be given in numbers, 'the ball carried 100 yards,' or words, 'at the top of your backswing, your left wrist was flat.' Just as precise numerical feedback is beneficial for learning, verbal feedback should be specific as well. Hearing 'good shot' tells you it was a good shot in someone's opinion, but it does not give you any constructive information about why or how it was good. When you give feedback, avoid negative or don't statements. Instead, describe the solution and what to do differently in an actionable way. As a player, if you receive feedback that is not clear and helpful, ask for it to be more specific so that you know exactly what you need to do differently.

Check Your Understanding

If you're coaching someone, always ask them to explain their understanding of your feedback. We often presume our feedback is clear, but this isn't always the case, so it's best to check. The meaning of your message is the response you get. Often this is not as you had intended so you will need to find a different way to say the same thing.

As a player, explain in your own words your interpretation of what you are trying to do and check your coach agrees with your understanding. This can save many weeks of wasted practice and frustration.

Recall

Make a habit of writing down key feelings or movements you are trying to master. This creates an association between your feedback and how you understand it, and it should make it easier for you to reconnect with the feedback later. Make sure your wording is clear so if you refer to your notes in 6 months or a year, it is still easy to understand.

Mistakes Can Help You

Golf is hard, and no one has mastered it yet. Mistakes are not an indication of a lack of skill; they are normal and an important part of learning because we learn the most from making mistakes and trying to correct them. If you don't struggle, you will not improve. Michael Jordan famously said, "I've missed more than 9000 shots in my career. I've lost almost 300 games. Twenty-six times, I've been trusted to take the game-winning shot and missed. I've failed over and over and over again in my life. And that is why I succeed."

Learn from your mistakes so you make them less often, and be realistic with your shot expectations. Perfectionist traits can rapidly kill the fun and enjoyment of playing golf, and how you react to and recover from mistakes massively influences your performances and scores. To get better, you must practice every shot including your weaker ones. We too often prefer to practice what we are good at, but when we struggle, we grow. Be prepared to make mistakes, and use the feedback to learn and improve.

PERFORMANCE

Routines

Concentration

We can all concentrate, but we don't always focus on what will help us to play our best golf. One of the biggest challenges we face is learning to focus our attention on what we can control. Time has 3 parts: past, present and future. Your body is always in the present, but your brain can jump between the past, present and future at any time. If you are thinking about something that has already happened or thinking ahead to what might happen, unwanted outcomes are more likely. When you are in the present and solely focused on your current task, your mind and body tend to be more in sync. In this state, you create the best opportunity to hit a great shot.

It is difficult to maintain concentration for a practice session or 18 holes, so it is helpful to have strategies to set your focus and bring you into the present before a shot. Creating routines to follow before, during and after every shot will give you the best opportunity to establish a stable equilibrium and play your best golf.

Dr Nicky Lumb & Dr Dave Alred MBE

Decisions and Strategy

To consistently achieve low scores, you need to have a good strategy, make smart decisions and be able to hit shots that match your intention. In competitions, once you arrive at your ball, you have 40 seconds to evaluate the situation, choose the most appropriate shot, select the club, go through your pre-shot routine and hit the ball. Sometimes forty seconds will be plenty of time, yet on other occasions, you may feel rushed. A 100-yard shot from a good lie to a flag in the middle of a green is going to require less thought than a 150-yard shot from a poor lie to an island green on a windy day.

At times, being overly optimistic can lead to poor, unrealistic decisions. On challenging holes where there are big water carries, there can be a temptation to try to carry the water and pull off a shot you would only make once in every twenty or thirty attempts. Whilst it's great to have so much confidence, it's usually best to play the higher percentage shot, unless there are exceptional circumstances to justify your decision, such as needing to make a birdie to force a playoff in a championship.

The circumstances within a round can influence decisions. At times, making them can feel easy. At other times, doubt and uncertainty can cause us to struggle even with a seemingly straightforward decision. Jean Van de Velde was in this situation playing the 72nd hole of the 1999 Open Championship at Carnoustie. Needing a double bogey to win, Van de Velde drove the final fairway. His second shot to the green hit a fairway grandstand and bounced into knee-high rough. His third shot finished in a creek. Disconcerted, he took his shoes and socks off whilst trying to decide whether to play the shot or take a penalty drop. He finished the hole with a triple bogey. This put him into a three-way playoff with Justin Leonard and Paul Lawrie, which Lawrie went on to win.

Traditionally, golf practice involves hitting balls on the driving range with the same club to the same target. When you are learning a new movement, this can be helpful, but it does not prepare you for the decisions you must make before every shot on the course. Sometimes these will be in highly pressurized situations. With weather and course conditions always changing, it's important to become proficient at evaluating different shot options and to continuously develop your tactical skills. The more decisions you make, the more familiar you will become with their expected outcome, and the better choices you will start to make. You will also absorb relevant information faster, and more decisions will become subconscious and automatic.

Low scores are often accomplished by choosing the right shot at the right time. They are not just achieved on days when you are hitting the ball well. When you are not at your best, a good strategy and structured decision-making process will help you to think smartly. It will give you the best opportunity to sensibly plot your way around a course while keeping your ball in play and achieving the lowest possible score.

Dr Nicky Lumb & Dr Dave Alred MBE

Shot Pattern

A shot pattern is the dispersion of shots from left to right and short to long. Knowing the size, distribution and centre of your shot patterns as well as how far an average shot lands from a target can help you to choose the most appropriate targets. Most golfers aim for the middle of the fairway off the tee and at the flag on their approach shots into greens, but often these targets are not in the middle of their shot patterns, so they take avoidable risks. During competitive rounds, it's rare for the world's best players to aim at many, if any, flags. Instead, they train themselves to choose their own targets, which are often in the middle of their shot patterns, so that they more effectively plot their way around the course.

By knowing your carry distances, shot patterns and average proximity to targets with every club, you can better evaluate the risk and reward of different shot options. Sometimes a conservative, damage-limiting shot is a better strategic option than trying to pull off a high-risk shot of a lifetime. As a general guide, if you feel you could successfully execute a shot seven times out of ten, then go for it! But if not, choose a more conservative target. Lower scores are usually achieved by dropping fewer shots, not by making more birdies.

If an average shot with a 7 iron flies 150 yards and finishes 20 feet left of the target, then choosing and hitting to a target 20 feet right of the flag will see more shots finishing closer to the hole. If there is out of bounds or water on the left, then aiming 30 feet right reduces further risk. Playing smart golf means choosing targets you can more easily recover from if you have slight mishits. If a fairway is 40 yards wide and out of bounds is 10 yards left of it, then depending on the size and centre of your shot pattern, choose a target on the right side of the fairway or even in the right rough. By fully committing to a target in the middle of your shot pattern, you will reduce the possibility of your ball going out of bounds, and even if you don't hit the shot you intended, your ball should still be in play.

To calculate the size and shape of your shot patterns, use one club to hit at least 10 shots towards a directional target (the more shots, the better). Discard any really poor shots by hitting another ball, but leave in slight mishits, so you have at least 10 balls that represent your average shots, not just your best 10.

Pace out the shot length and distance from the target of each ball, and mark their locations in your notebook. Draw around the outside of all of the shots to create your shot pattern. This will enable you to calculate its length, width and middle, plus your average shot distance and proximity to the target. Repeat this exercise with every club so you can fill in the shot matrix chart. To make your numbers as accurate as possible, walk to the putting green between every shot, hole a four-foot putt and then walk back to play your next shot, so that there is time and variation between each shot, just like there would be on the course. If you have access to a launch monitor, it will do all of the calculations for you and save a lot of time.

Dr Nicky Lumb & Dr Dave Alred MBE

Most golfers' shot patterns get bigger as their clubs get longer. With irons, shot patterns are usually a tilted oval shape for a right-handed player, with shots to the left going further due to a slightly closed (left-pointing) club face and less loft at impact. Shots to the right usually have a more open (right-pointing) club face which increases loft and reduces distance. This means when a flag is back left or front right, you can be slightly more aggressive with your shots.

Once you have a better understanding of your shot data, you will be able to choose targets on the course which best suit your game. As your shots become more accurate, you will notice your shot patterns reducing in size and the shot centre moving nearer to your actual target.

Decision-Making Process

Practice going through the decision-making process and hitting within forty seconds. Score the decision and result of each shot. Quantifying your success will help you to learn and make better decisions in the future.

Step	Considerations	Decision
1. Shot Distance	• What is the distance to the front of the green and target? • How far is the flag from the front and back of the green?	
2. Evaluate the Lie	• How is the ball lying? • Can you achieve a clean strike? • With a poor lie, which club will give you the best chance of good contact?	
3. Evaluate Target Landing Area	• Where's the flag on the green? • Where are the safest areas (short, long, left, right)? • How will the ball react on landing (will it run or stop quickly)? • Where is the best landing spot? Choose a small, precise target. • What is the distance?	

Dr Nicky Lumb & Dr Dave Alred MBE

Step	Considerations	Decision

4. Evaluate Weather	• **Wind / Distance**
	  ◦ Will the wind affect the ball flight?
	  ◦ If yes, will the ball go shorter or further?
	  ◦ By how much?
	• **Wind / Direction**
	  ◦ Will the wind affect the shot's direction?
	  ◦ If yes, will the ball move left or right?
	  ◦ By how much?	

5. Expectation	• What is your average proximity to the target from this distance? • What is your shot shape? • What is your usual shot pattern? • Where should you aim? • What is the club?	
6. Intention	• Target • Club • Distance to Landing Spot • Playing Distance to Landing Spot • Shot Shape and Flight	

Figure 10. Shot Decision Making Process

Warning!

The decision-making chart may seem a bit complex, but it is providing you with a process list to cover all eventualities so you can carefully plan and prepare for every shot. When using it, take the time to fill it out accurately. This will help you to ingrain the process until it becomes second nature.

Pre-Shot Routine

A pre-shot routine is a series of processes that join together to form a simple but engaging to-do list of thoughts and actions which you can follow before every shot. It can help you to be more consistent in how you mentally and physically plan, prepare and execute each shot. All of the processes within your pre-shot routine must be doable and if possible measurable so you can always evaluate how well you completed them. At his peak, Tiger Woods would take the same amount of time to hit every shot. It did not matter whether he was in contention to win a major championship or fighting to make the cut; his routine was always the same. The more consistent your pre-shot routine is in its duration, number of practice swings, number of looks at the target and time you stand over the ball before you start your backswing, the better prepared your mind and body are likely to be.

Developing your own individualised pre-shot routine is important, as everyone is unique. Once you have discovered what works best for you, apply your routine to every shot on the course and to all or a high proportion of off-course shots so that it becomes a repeatable and automatic process.

On the course, pressures can build quickly, especially when you are playing below your handicap or are in contention to win an event. Having a routine brings some certainty into situations that can feel uncomfortable. Although the results of shots will vary, your pre-shot routine should stay the same. Following your routine and committing to perform

Dr Nicky Lumb & Dr Dave Alred MBE

it to the best of your ability means you are doing your best on every shot, and that is all you can ask of yourself. The better you are at executing your routine and the processes within it, the more likely you are to match your shot's intentions and achieve lower scores. You cannot control what others do, but you can control what you do.

Self-Talk

The way you speak, especially to yourself (self-talk) before, during and after a shot, can increase or decrease your confidence and influence how you feel and behave on your next shot. If you think, 'avoid the out of bounds on the left,' then it's likely your ball will go left and out of bounds or miles right to compensate. Rather than using negative phrasing, tell yourself what to do and exactly where you want the ball to go.

Self-talk can be uplifting and can increase your focus and productivity. Look for the positives in every situation, and be constructive in your language by giving yourself 'to do' instructions. It is frustrating to hit a disappointing shot, but rather than beating yourself up, be neutral and objective.

'The shot did not match my intention, but I am going to make my next shot great by really sticking to my routine.'

No one likes to be told off, so don't do it to yourself. Instead be front-footed and start planning your next great shot. Always focus on building yourself up by congratulating yourself when you do something well and forgiving any mistakes. This is very effective but often tough to do!

Start by identifying your self-talk, and then work on reframing any negative words or thoughts so you become a master in positive and productive dialogue. The Self-Talk practice on page 132 will help you to do this. When Tiger Woods was growing up, it's reported he used this affirmation as he walked around the course.

I will my own destiny.
I believe in me.
I smile at obstacles.
I am firm in my resolve.
I fulfil my resolutions powerfully.
My strength is great.
I stick to it, easily, naturally.
My will moves mountains.
I focus and give it my all.
My decisions are strong.
I do it all with my heart.

I love the challenge of this game!

Be Big and Powerful

Your posture and body language can influence how you think and feel. If you stand tall, with your shoulders back, head up and eyes looking forward, your blood flow increases and your brain receives more oxygen. This makes you feel more alert, confident and powerful. In contrast, when you feel weak, fearful or uncertain, you do the opposite and round your shoulders, becoming smaller and subservient.

Dr Nicky Lumb & Dr Dave Alred MBE

Amy Cuddy, one of the world's leading researchers in body language and power posing, suggests that standing in a powerful position with your body expansive and stretched out for two minutes alters your brain and body chemistry and helps you to feel more confident. It increases your levels of testosterone, one of the dominant hormones in your body, and reduces cortisol, a stress hormone. This makes you feel more powerful and in control.

Although you do not have two minutes before you hit every shot to adopt a power pose, the way you position your body will influence how you feel and perform. As part of your pre-shot routine, think 'be powerful' and take up as much space as possible, so you feel physically 'big.' Doing this as you walk around the course will also benefit your performance. The Body Language practice on page 134 will encourage you to do this.

Swing Key(s)

Swing keys are thoughts, feelings or images based on the process of hitting a ball. Most golfers have them to reinforce something technically specific that will help them to produce their best shots. It's important to discover which keys work best for you as the same one will not work for everyone. You may decide to have a key for standing over the ball and another during your swing, but keep them to a minimum so they are not overburdening and make sure they are clear, simple and engaging. They should give you an external focus of attention as well.

A pre-swing key could be to check your club face is pointing at the target or to push the soles of your shoes into the ground so that you are evenly balanced. An in-swing thought could be to get your belt buckle to point at the target before the top button on your shirt in your downswing or to crush the ball with the club face to promote a good strike.

100% Commitment

Before every shot, you must have a clear, simple plan and be fully committed to it. If any doubts or second thoughts enter your mind, always stop, logically re-evaluate the situation and only restart your hitting process once you are fully committed to the shot you have decided to play.

In some situations, the most appropriate shot will be obvious, but at other times, it will require more thought. Through practice, you will find you are more accurate and confident playing certain shots than others. On the course, especially when you are performing under pressure, always play the shot you feel most confident playing, even if you feel it isn't necessarily the most logical one to play. A shot decision that is 80% correct but 100% committed to is much better than a 100% correct decision that is only 80% committed to.

Playing a shot you can see and feel and are 100% committed to is good decision-making. This does not mean you will always be successful, but playing a shot half-heartedly or worrying if you can actually make it will distract you from playing well. Always play the best shot for you.

Dr Nicky Lumb & Dr Dave Alred MBE

The Commitment practice on page 130 will help you to do this.

Target

In Harvey Penick's Little Red Book, the author uses the term 'take dead aim' to get his players to see exactly where they want the ball to go. He suggests, 'Take dead aim at a spot on the fairway or on the green... Make it a point to do it every time on every shot. Don't just do it from time to time, when you happen to remember. Take dead aim.' Aiming at the smallest possible target has the greatest focus effect.

Sometimes we see a big, open fairway and hit a ball without any thought. Moments later, we wonder how we missed such a wide target with our ball now resting in heavy rough. In practice, we often take a similar approach and hit shots without aiming at a specific target. To improve, always aim at the smallest possible target. This could be a leaf, part of a tree branch or trunk, a discoloured piece of grass on a green or even the pin itself. Never use negative phrasing such as 'don't go left,' to avoid something. Instead, see exactly where you want the ball to go, pick out a small, precise target, aim at it and strike! If you want to hit a barn door every time, aim for the key hole! The practice on page 126 will encourage you to do this on every shot.

Intention

To play your best golf, have a plan for every ball you hit. This often leads to more favourable outcomes and can help you to objectively assess if a shot went well. It's difficult to judge whether a shot matched your intention if you did not decide where you wanted the ball to go or how you wanted it to get there. Having a clear purpose and target can help you to learn from each shot, so you can make the next one better. The Set your Intention practice on page 128 will help you to set a clear intention for every shot.

Visualise the Shot

To give yourself the best opportunity of hitting a great shot, create a picture in your mind of the shot you want to play so that your brain knows exactly what you want the ball to do.

Stand behind the ball and picture it flying from its starting point with the intended shape and trajectory to where you want it to land and finish. If it is difficult for you to see the whole flight, imagine a laser beam going from your ball to the target or just stare at the target with tunnel vision. The more clarity you have with your intention, the more likely you are to achieve it.

Full-Dress Rehearsal

Once you have a clear picture of the shot you are going to play, it is time to prepare your body. Most tour players take two practice swings which are either exact copies of their

Dr Nicky Lumb & Dr Dave Alred MBE

intended swing or involve a swing that reinforces a specific move or feel, followed by an exact copy of their intended swing. As you complete your full-dress rehearsal, imagine the feel of the ball coming off your club face, hear the club face perfectly striking the ball, and see the ball flying and landing at its intended target. This will deepen your awareness and strengthen your mental connection to the shot.

Aim and Alignment

Stand behind the ball looking towards the target. Picture the shot you are going to play. See the line you want the ball to start on. When you approach the ball, align your club face to the target. If you prefer to line up to something closer to you, choose an intermediary target such as a leaf, divot or discoloured piece of grass that's one to two feet in front of the ball and in line with the target.

Now set your body so that your feet, hips and shoulders are parallel to the ball-to-target line. If you imagine a set of railway tracks, then your ball-to-target line will be on the right track and your body will be on the left. If you are going to shape the shot or have your own alignment preferences and don't want to stand square to the target, set your club face and body accordingly, but make sure you are appropriately aligned. Good alignment is crucial in getting the ball to consistently go where you want it to.

Steady Eyes

When you are standing over the ball, a consistent approach in the way your eyes locate the target and then aim can help you to hit better shots. Fixing your eyes on a specific spot or dimple on the ball just before the start of a swing keeps your eyes still, head controlled and gives your brain time to process the information it has received about the shot you want to play. The brain can then plan the motion and instruct your body in how to make the swing. Once you have addressed the ball, the more your eyes move, the more active your brain is and the greater the chance of distraction. In contrast, steady eyes usually means a quieter brain, fewer distractions and as a result better shots. If you hold your gaze for too long, your mind is more likely to wander, so keep the time over the ball short and sweet.

This principle is similar for putting. To incorporate it into your routine once you have selected your line and speed, look at the ball, then move your eyes to the precise spot where you want the ball to go. Take a snapshot of the target in your mind, and hold your gaze for a second or two, then go back to the ball and focus on it. Look at the target again and check the snapshot in your mind. Go back to the ball, fix your eyes on a spot or dimple on the back of the ball that you want the putter face to strike, and then, when you are ready, start your stroke. Fixing your eyes on the ball before, during and after a putt increases the chances of making a good putt and being able to do this while keeping a picture of the target in your mind's eye is one of golf's ultimate skills. Poor putters often look up to see where the

Dr Nicky Lumb & Dr Dave Alred MBE

ball has finished before they have hit it, which results in less accurate putts.

See it, Feel it, Do it!

Once you are correctly aligned over the ball, it is time to let your subconscious take over. You are focused on the shot, are aware of your senses and have little or no outside interference. Ideally, you will have no technical thoughts, just possibly one or two swing keys or feelings. Crucially, your mind and body know what they are about to do, and it is time to do it. A couple of waggles and final looks at the target may be needed, and then it's time to settle your eyes on the ball and fire!

Keep the time you stand over the ball to a minimum so that it reduces any potential distractions. To do this, try to always be preparing to do, or actually doing something mentally or physically, so that you are never just stood over the ball waiting.

Post-Shot Routine

Evaluating Your Shots

A good shot does not always mean a good scoring result. Sometimes, you will meticulously follow your pre-shot routine and hit the shot you intended to, only for the wind to pick up whilst your ball is airborne. Or your ball could bounce unfavourably on landing and finish in a difficult position. A well-struck putt can roll well, travel on its intended line at the desired speed, and not drop into the hole. Exactly where your ball finishes is not always predictable or controllable. It's important to evaluate the success of your shots on how well you complete your pre-shot routine and the processes you work to, not just on where the ball finishes. If you can focus your attention and judge your performances on what you can control, you are more likely to get favourable outcomes and be in control of how you measure a shot's success.

Score Your Routine

Your routines are one of the few factors you can control. Immediately after hitting a shot, score yourself out of 10 on how well you completed one of the processes within your pre-shot routine, without being influenced by the outcome of the shot. Once this becomes a habit, add another process to score, and over time add more, until you are scoring all of the processes most relevant to you or giving your routine an overall score. These can include;

Dr Nicky Lumb & Dr Dave Alred MBE

1. How precise was your target selection?

2. How vividly did you visualise the shot and set your intention?

3. How committed were you to the shot?

4. How well did the shot match your intention?

5. Score your self-talk, was it positive and productive?

6. Score your body language / posture, was it big and powerful?

The pre-shot process scorecard on page 297 will help you to record your scores after every shot. At the end of a round, total the results, calculate your average score per shot and record it so you can monitor your scores over time. You will start to see that as your process scores increase, your playing scores will decrease. A long-term goal should be to try and achieve 10/10 on every process.

Shot Reaction

"*It's not what happens to golfers, but how they choose to respond to what happens that distinguishes champions.*" - Bob Rotella.

We always want to hit good shots, but disappointing shots are inevitable, and how we react to them can make or break a round. How many times have you seen a playing partner mutter under their breath, shout at themselves or slam a club into their bag after a shot? A picture can paint a thousand words, and so often a player's body language instantly shows how they think they are playing. The way you mentally manage yourself after a disappointing shot can be the difference between finishing first or second, winning or losing, or saving an increase in your handicap. After all, one poor shot can only cost a maximum of two shots. It's how you react after this that can either save or ruin your round. The ultimate post-shot reaction is the last shot never happened.

On the 13th tee of the final round in the 2017 Open Championship, Jordan Spieth was tied for the lead when he hit a wayward drive to the right. After declaring his ball unplayable, Spieth took a drop about 70 yards behind where his ball originally lay. His next shot finished short and to the right of the green, but he got up and down, and in the end, he only dropped one shot. He then played the remaining five holes in an incredible five under par to win his first Open Championship. Jordan Spieth had the mental discipline to not let one poor drive spoil his round. Instead, he accepted the mistake, swiftly moved on and used it to inspire him to play better. Part of golf is how well you recover from a disappointing shot. Are you able to move on to the next hole without letting a dropped shot affect you, or is it more likely to create mental turmoil and destroy your round?

How Do You React After a Shot?

After every shot, you can have a positive, negative or neutral reaction, and this can make or break your round. You cannot control your scores or the exact outcome of a shot, but you can always control how you react. Your

Dr Nicky Lumb & Dr Dave Alred MBE

thoughts, beliefs and behaviours have patterns. One of the advantages of creating pressure and scoring shots during your practice is that it makes you more aware of your tendencies and gives you the opportunity to identify, manage and improve how you react to them. Having a routine to follow after every shot can help neutralise any negative emotions so you perform closer to your best on the next one.

Be Neutral or Positive

After each shot, aim to be neutral or positive. If you followed your routine and achieved a high process score, congratulate yourself on this regardless of the shot's outcome. Achieving a high process score shows you focused on what you could control. If your process score was low, set yourself the challenge of achieving a better process score on your next shot.

If the ball finishes in a disappointing position or hits something and bounces badly, learn to accept it. It has happened, and there is nothing you can do about it. Be productive and ask yourself, 'what can I do differently?' The odds are in your favour that the next shot will be better, so tell yourself, 'I have a great shot coming up!'

To become more aware of and to improve your post-shot reactions, play a game against yourself and award two points every time you have a positive reaction after a shot, one point for a neutral reaction, and subtract three points for a negative reaction. Keep records of these games, and over time, see how high you can make your score.

The Mental Recovery Process

If you feel yourself starting to get frustrated, it is helpful to have processes you can follow that will help you to reset and be in the best possible state to play your next shot. Try these techniques, see which ones work best for you, and then score how well you can apply them out of 10 after each shot. The scorecard on page 298 will help you to record your scores during a round and monitor them over time.

Erase It

Immediately after your shot, make a practice swing and emphasise the movement you wanted to make so you give yourself the best opportunity for your next shot to match your intention.

Look Up

Reset by looking up and focusing above the flag stick. If you are on the green and the flag is out of the hole, set your eyes to the top of the tree line. Where the eyes go, the body follows, so set your gaze, lift your head up and make your body feel big and powerful by taking up as much physical space as possible.

Pause

Stand and pause for a few seconds so your rational mind can catch up. Count up to 5000 in thousands. Start with 1000 Mississippi, 2000 Mississippi and so on.

Dr Nicky Lumb & Dr Dave Alred MBE

Breathe

Slowly count to five as you breathe in, then count to seven as you breathe out. Do five of these and keep going if necessary. Breathing out for longer than you breathe in helps to lower your heart rate. By focusing on your breath, there is less opportunity for something else to distract you. Slowly clenching and unclenching your fists as you do this can help your body to relax and calm down.

Count

Slowly start counting backwards from 1000. If you feel you need more distraction, then start subtracting in multiples of 7.

Words

You can talk yourself into or out of almost anything, so talk yourself into making your next shot great. Repeat the affirmation, 'I am going to really follow my pre-shot routine, fully commit to the shot and completely match my intention. My next shot is going to be great.'

How Do You React After a Great Shot?

At times, we can be so excited after hitting a great shot that our minds race ahead, we lose concentration, and we don't make the most of the opportunity to create some momentum. Have you ever hit a perfect drive, had a much shorter shot than normal into the green and then hit a disappointing approach shot that missed the green? Or hit a great second shot to the green on a par 5, only to miss several putts and walk off the green disappointed? It's only when the ball is in the hole that a great shot really counts. Being aware of potential distractions and training yourself to focus on your processes can help you to capitalise on the opportunities you create.

Congratulate Yourself

Our brains handle positive and negative information differently. We tend to react more strongly to unfavourable stimuli because of our brain's inherent fight-or-flight mechanism. We also remember negative emotions for longer and in more detail. This means that a bad shot will always have a greater impact than a good shot. As a basic rule, we remember three negatives to one positive, and a setback makes us three times more dissatisfied than our progress helps to please us. This means we need to hit three good shots to erase the memory of one poor shot. We therefore have to work much harder at reinforcing what we do well. To do this, note every time you do something well and write it down, so that you gather an ever-increasing collection of positive memories and achievements.

Goal Setting

Getting better takes time and requires persistence, determination and a lot of hard work. Aiming to be better every day can help you to feel you are always moving forwards, and goal setting can help you to do this. When

Dr Nicky Lumb & Dr Dave Alred MBE

you set a goal, you usually perform better than when you simply try to do your best, so it's most productive to always have goals you want to achieve. There are three key types of goals: outcome goals, performance goals and process goals.

Outcome goals are usually based on tournament results such as winning a championship, so they involve comparing your scores to others. This means that you can play your best golf but not achieve your goal because someone else shot lower scores. Achieving an outcome goal is not under your control.

In contrast, performance goals are controllable by you, and these can form the building blocks towards achieving your ultimate goals. Performance goals involve breaking your game into skills and trying to improve each one. A performance goal could be to improve the percentage of putts holed between 3 and 10 feet from 25% to 30% or to get up and down at least 25% of the time from between 10 and 20 yards. Performance goals can give your practice a competitive edge and make you more accountable for your shots. They can also create games within games as you can work to improve your scores within each skill set during your rounds. The key factor is you have complete control.

Process goals focus on how to achieve your performance and outcome goals, and again are under your full control. A process goal could be to only hit a shot once you have selected a precise target or to always walk away from a shot and reset if any doubt enters your mind. Committing to achieving a good roll on the ball with every putt is another on-course process goal. In practice, you could commit to practicing putts between 3 and 10 feet for 10 minutes every day or to make 25 practice swings each morning, reinforcing a specific swing movement, before you leave your home.

The Goal-Setting Process

The following steps can help to make your goal setting most effective:

1. Write down all of your goals.

2. Be specific about what you want to achieve. Wanting to reduce your handicap is not specific, but a goal to get to a single-digit handicap of nine is.

3. Set goals that are important to you and which will bring purpose to your practice. Write them in the present tense and use affirmative words, 'Today I am going to fully commit to my pre-shot routine before every shot. If I do this I have a great opportunity to win the club championship this year. Within 5 years, I could well be playing off scratch.'

4. To get better, you need a starting point. Break your game into different skills, and identify your current skill levels using numbers so that you can monitor your progress over time. The practices in the Know your Game and Your Expectations sections on pages 115 and 101 will help you to do this.

5. Set a completion date or at least check point dates for your goals. You are more likely to achieve them if you have a deadline.

Dr Nicky Lumb & Dr Dave Alred MBE

6.   Your goals should be stepping stones to get you where you want to go. If you feel a goal is no longer relevant, immediately adapt it.

A performance diary can help monitor your actions on a daily basis, reduce the likelihood of distractions, and lead to the fastest improvement gains. The No Limits Performance Programme is an excellent resource for this (www.dairmagazine.com).

Goal-Setting Example

Answering the following questions will help you to set your goals and make your practice time productive. The examples demonstrate how to set clear, specific goals.

What is your ultimate long-term goal?
Win the club championship – Outcome Goal

List a goal which will help you to reach your ultimate long-term goal that you can achieve:

In your next practice session:
Practice my 3-10ft putting and set a new personal best of -6 (33%).

By the end of the week:
Complete at least three 3-10ft putting practices and achieve a new personal best of -7 (39%).

By the end of the month:
Complete at least three 3-10ft putting practices each week and achieve a new personal best of -8 (44%).

By the end of the year:
Improve my 3-10ft putting and achieve a new personal best of -10 (56%).

Repeat this process for the skill sets that will reduce your scores the most.

Celebrate Achievements

All of your actions have a cumulative effect on your progress and ultimate success. Setting small, measurable goals that are just beyond your current abilities and trying to achieve them on a daily basis is motivating. As soon as you achieve a goal, set a new one that is harder and just out of reach, so that your goals act as stepping stones towards achieving your ultimate goal.

Every time you achieve a goal, celebrate your success. When you anticipate or reach an achievement, your body releases dopamine, the 'happy drug.' This gives you a sense of satisfaction, so you want more of it. With dream goals usually years away from being fulfilled, it's constructive to set goals you can achieve on a regular basis—ideally during every practice session, providing you perform well. The more success you have, the more successful you will see yourself as being. This has a cumulative effect on building momentum and pushing you to get better, and it ensures you frequently get a dopamine boost.

Dr Nicky Lumb & Dr Dave Alred MBE

Confidence

Confidence is one of the most important psychological attributes you can possess. It influences how you feel, what you think, what you say, how you behave and what you do. It hugely affects how you play and react on the course. When you are confident, you feel optimistic and in control, you expect to play well and your expectations become a self-fulfilling prophecy: you become what you think you will become. If you believe you can hit a great shot, then you probably can, but if you think you can't, then you probably won't.

Some players see great performances and confidence as temporary. If they are shooting low scores and winning, they feel confident, but if their scores are high, they don't. This is an outcome-orientated approach and difficult to systematically achieve, because if you are not producing low scores, then it suggests that your confidence will not increase. It is also contradictory because you can play well and score poorly and play badly and score well. For long-term progress, it's best to create methodical processes that you can follow and control which will gradually increase your confidence over time.

Building Your Confidence

Process vs. Outcome

If you assess your performances on victory or defeat, then your confidence will be affected every time you don't win. In

2016, CBS Sports reported that Tiger Woods's career win ratio on the PGA Tour was 24.2%, with Rory McIlroy next at 9.91%, and Jordan Spieth third at 8.16%. This meant that Woods was winning once in every four or five attempts, and he is arguably the greatest golfer of all time. If professional golfers were to base their confidence on victories, then they would not be very confident, so don't make this mistake. You cannot control a tournament result or what others do, but you can control what you do, so focus your attention on your own actions. Building pre-competition, pre-shot and post-shot routines so that they become automatic is one of the most productive ways of taking control of your actions and increasing your confidence.

Facts

Facts are what you achieve. They are evidence of your hard work and successes. Writing down what you have accomplished on a daily basis is building facts, and looking back at them over a week, month or year should give you a positive outlook on what you have achieved and how much you have improved. You can create facts anywhere; on the course, chipping or putting green, on the driving range or in the gym, just make sure you take the time and effort to identify them and write them down!

Past Performance

Positive past performances and achievements build confidence. Write down your previous achievements in competition and practice and keep your list up to date so

Dr Nicky Lumb & Dr Dave Alred MBE

that you can always refer back to your successes. If you've accomplished something once, then you can do it again!

Vicarious Experience

You can gain confidence from watching and learning what others do, and sometimes observing what not to do. Seeing friends work towards their goals and then achieve them can help you to accomplish yours, as you will see that realising your goals is achievable. If they can do it, so can you!

Language

You can talk yourself into and out of anything. Always use positive and productive words, and focus on what you want to do rather than what you want to avoid. Working hard on improving your self-talk can dramatically build your confidence and self-esteem.

Dopamine

When you know your skill levels have increased and you feel more capable and confident in your abilities, your body releases more dopamine. This improves your concentration, helps you to learn faster and enables you to process feedback more effectively, so building your confidence means that you gain in every way.

Realistic Expectations

Score Inconsistency

Most of us have had days when everything 'clicked.' Shots finished closer to their targets than usual, putts dropped, and you achieved your best scores. On other days, everything was a struggle and it felt as if you've never played golf before. Shots went off line, others took bad bounces, and putts charged past the hole. These contrasting rounds can happen within a few hours of each other, yet what changed?

This natural inconsistency is a challenge we face as humans, since we are unable to operate as reliable machines. Golf at every level is a game of inconsistency. If you look at the scores of the world's best players over a season, you will see large fluctuations. In 2018, Justin Rose, Dustin Johnson and Brooks Koepka were all ranked number 1 in the world. On the PGA Tour in 2018, Justin Rose's scoring average was 68.9. His lowest score was 63, and his highest was 74, so his best and worst round scores differed by 11 shots. Dustin Johnson's scoring average was 68.69. His lowest score was 63, and his highest was 77, a difference of 14 shots. Brooks Koepka's scoring average was 69.4. His lowest round was 63, and his highest was 78, a difference of 15 shots. These large variations show how difficult it is to always score well. If the world's best players experience such variations over a season, then lower-ranked professionals, elite amateurs and club golfers should expect and accept much bigger differences.

Dr Nicky Lumb & Dr Dave Alred MBE

Perception and the TV Effect

Watching golf on the TV makes the world's best players look superhuman. We see players hitting most fairways, firing iron shots close to flags, and holing many putts. TV coverage favours the players who are in contention to win and rarely broadcasts the many players who are struggling to make the cut. Tour professionals are phenomenal golfers. If they play an average members' course that's about 6400 yards, they would expect to shoot in the very low 60s and be at least 7 or 8 under par. However, most tour professionals make approximately 80% of their annual on-course earnings from 3 or 4 events a year. For the rest of their season, they are grinding it out like every other golfer, just at a much higher level, and one most players dream of achieving. No one scores well all of the time, and most shots do not go exactly where you want them to.

One of the biggest skills in golf is accepting that it's inevitable that shots will not always match your intention. Once you understand that committing to your routines is the only part of a shot you can control, it is much easier to accept a shot's outcome. Developing this robust mindset will help you play your best golf.

Your Expectations

How many times have you been frustrated when you missed a green or didn't hole an 8-foot putt? Setting realistic expectations can make it easier to manage your emotions, reduce your frustrations and increase your enjoyment on the course. A PGA Tour player hits an average of 12 greens in regulation per round (67%). A 10 handicap player hits around 7 greens in regulation (just under 40%) while an 18 handicap player hits between 4 and 5 greens (approximately 25%) per round. A PGA Tour player holes an average of 53% of 8-foot putts. This means that the best players in the world usually miss one 8-foot putt and then hole the next. Yet how often do you see club golfers turn away in disgust or mutter an expletive when they miss a green or an 8-foot putt doesn't drop into the hole?

Calculating your accuracy will give you factual information about your game and can help you to be realistic with your shot expectations which usually gives golfers more satisfaction when they are playing. On the putting green, if you attempt ten different 8-foot putts, how many would you expect to hole? If you make two and miss eight, your success rate would be 20%, and you should at best expect to hole 20% on the course. This may be a sobering thought but it will help you to be more realistic with your shot expectations and as a result mentally tougher.

The chart below shows the main shot categories that contribute to a total score at the end of a round. For club golfers many of the longer approach shots will not be relevant. The leading score in each shot category on the PGA Tour is listed first, followed by the tour average. You will see that amongst the world's best players there can be big differences in their skill levels. It's most accurate to determine your current skill levels by recording and then analysing your on-course playing statistics. There are

Dr Nicky Lumb & Dr Dave Alred MBE

many apps and online platforms that can analyse your data once you have collected it. Golf Metrics, designed by Mark Broadie, is one of the best. If you prefer to do your calculations manually the analysis chart on page 295 will help you.

An alternative would be to calculate your scores during practice by hitting 10 shots from random places in each shot category and working out your averages. To get the truest representation of your game, measure two or three shot categories at the same time. For example, cycle from one 3ft putt, to a chip from a random position between 10 and 20 yards, and then to an iron shot between 125 and 150 yards. It's important to do it in this context because if you have ten different three-foot putts in a row, you are likely to hole more of them than if you had to walk to the driving range and hit a drive between each one. Once you know your scores, you will have a baseline and can set goals to improve them. You can also be realistic with your shot expectations on and off the course.

Putting				
Putts Made From	Highest Average	PGA Tour Average	Your Score	Your Goal
3-5ft	95%	87%		
5-10ft	67%	56%		
10-15ft	40%	30%		
15-20ft	30%	18%		
20-25ft	23%	13%		
> 25ft	10%	5%		

Off the Tee

Category	Highest Average	Tour Average	Your Score	Your Goal
Distance	318 yds	294 yds		
Fairways Hit	76%	62%		

Short Game

Distance to Hole	Proximity to Hole			
	Best Average	PGA Tour Average	Your Score	Your Goal
< 10yds	2ft	4ft		
10-20yds	6ft	7ft		
20-30yds	7ft	9ft		
> 30yds	8ft	12ft		
Sand Shots (Greenside Bunkers)	7ft	10ft		

Up and Downs

Distance to Hole	Highest Average	Tour Average	Your Score	Your Goal
< 10yds	97%	84%		
10-20yds	78%	64%		
20-30yds	70%	52%		
Sand Saves (Greenside Bunkers)	65%	50%		

Dr Nicky Lumb & Dr Dave Alred MBE

Distance to Hole	Proximity to Hole			Your Score (Fairway)	Your Goal
	Best	Tour Average	Rough**		
50-75yds	9ft	17ft	25ft		
75-100yds	13ft	18ft	27ft		
100-125yds	16ft	20ft	31ft		
125-150yds	18ft	23ft	37ft		
150-175yds	23ft	28ft	43ft		
175-200yds*	29ft	34ft	53ft		
200-225yds*	34ft	41ft	65ft		
225-250yds*	39ft	52ft	73ft		

Figure 11. PGA Tour players shot accuracy during the 2019 season.

*When you work out your proximity to the hole on approach shots only measure the yardage bands that are relevant to your game. Ignore the longer distances.

**The proximity to the hole from the rough is shown to illustrate the differences in accuracy when a player hits a shot into a green from the rough instead of the fairway.

(This chart uses proximity to the hole data from the PGA Tour. On the course players often aim for the safest part of a green and not the flag. A player could deliberately aim 20ft left of the flag, hit a shot that perfectly matches their intention, but the proximity to the hole statistic would be 20ft even though the ball finished at its intended position. Currently, it is not possible to know where a player is aiming on the course, so players may be more accurate than the statistics suggest).

Performing Under Pressure

When you are in a position to achieve a goal you really want, your desire to succeed often increases. Some golfers excel in these situations, but others struggle and play well below the standards they would expect in less pressurized situations. Often, this is because they start overthinking and trying too hard. They begin telling themselves how to swing the club or how to move a particular body part, wrongly believing that being more conscientious will reduce mistakes and increase the likelihood of them playing well and achieving their goal.

Unfortunately, this has the opposite effect as it disrupts the brain's normal thought patterns which can then interrupt a usually fluid swing. Thoughts that are normally subconscious and which should stay that way are instead unpicked by our anxiety to avoid failure. This can make a relatively straightforward shot feel much harder. Have you ever faced a flat four-foot putt to save par or win a competition that suddenly feels like a fast-breaking downhill ten-footer? Usually this happens when there is a significant consequence to missing the putt, even though it is mostly in your mind.

How you think, learn and practice will influence how you perform under pressure. The following tips can help you develop these important skills.

Dr Nicky Lumb & Dr Dave Alred MBE

Anxiety Can Be Excitement

Playing golf can be nerve-racking at times. How you manage your feelings will influence your performance. Anxiety is a state of nervousness or apprehension that occurs in the absence of real danger. It can create indecision, negative self-talk and loss of confidence, and it distracts you from following your usual routines. You may start overthinking or looking at things you would usually pay little or no attention to. In contrast, excitement is a feeling of enthusiasm and eagerness.

Ironically, anxiety and excitement are physiologically the same emotion. When you feel excited or anxious, your heart rate increases and adrenaline is released to prepare your muscles for exertion. This increases your ability to generate speed and power, which can lead to you hitting the ball much further with the same apparent effort. Off the tee, this can be helpful, but when you need to control the distance of your approach shots or play delicate chips to tricky flag positions, playing these shots effectively can be more challenging because your timing, coordination and movement control may change due to the energy rush.

Whilst some players struggle with these symptoms and start being cautious and trying to guide the ball, others perceive the sensations as an amazing energizing tool that will boost their performance and help them to excel. Because the effects of anxiety and excitement are interlinked, how you decide to interpret your feelings can have a big influence on your performance. View the sensations of butterflies in your stomach as your personal performance enhancer, and as soon as you feel yourself getting anxious, change your mindset by saying to yourself, 'I'm excited,' many times. Research by Dr Alison Wood Brooks at the Harvard Business School showed that repeatedly saying 'I'm excited' made people less anxious, more optimistic and better when performing under pressure, so let these words be your new performance drug!

What Do You Do Under Pressure?

When golfers are performing under pressure, their swings and behaviours can change. It's beneficial to know what your tendencies are, i.e. how and what changes. Do you usually strike the ball cleanly, or do you tend to thin the ball (hit the ball above its equator) or strike the ground before the ball? Does the ball usually fly straight or move from left to right or right to left? Does the curvature increase? On the greens, does the speed of your putts change? Do you leave putts short or charge them past the hole? Creating challenges with consequences during practice will help you to identify your tendencies and learn how to correct them, so you become more used to performing under pressure.

Learning

We learn in a variety of ways; by being told or shown what to do or by working it out for ourselves which through trial, error and repetition is often the deepest form of learning. Traditionally, coaches have instructed us in how to swing the club and play various shots. This results in

Dr Nicky Lumb & Dr Dave Alred MBE

us accumulating large amounts of information about our swings. This is effective for some short-term gains, but when you are competing in more stressful situations, there can be a temptation to start overthinking your swing technique. This has the potential to disrupt your usually fluent swings and as a result make your shots less accurate.

Discovery learning involves learning through trial and error. This results in you having less conscious knowledge about your swings and the way you play different shots, as your movements are more instinctive and rely on feel. In pressurized situations, shots that have been learned implicitly are often more effective as you are less likely to overthink them.

To play your best golf, you need a repeatable swing that allows you to hit the ball where you want it to go. Good technical knowledge can help you to achieve this, but the key is to be able to keep conscious technical thoughts to a minimum and become more target aware when you are playing, as well as during your training and tournament practice.

Metaphors

Metaphors are similarities between things which enable comparisons to be made. They are often used to create images / feelings that can be remembered without needing to refer back to detailed instructions. The key is to find something that you can already do very effectively and that has similarities with what you are trying to achieve.

For example, the analogy 'trace the face' created by Paul McGinley encourages the putter face to track to the hole which has the unconscious effect of keeping the putter face square to the target for longer. 'Chest logo to the target' helps to get your body through the ball so that you complete your swing with no mechanical thoughts.

Overcoming Overthinking

If you find yourself overthinking or trying to do too many things within your swing, practice in situations where you are unlikely to make mistakes so that the movements become more intuitive. This should help to quiet your mind. You are likely to give yourself fewer instructions if you are trying to improve your ball striking on one-foot putts rather than six-foot putts, as you will miss fewer times. Hitting into a net can help to overcome overthinking with your long game. The outcome of the shot is removed, so you can totally focus on the process of hitting the ball.

On the course, try to focus on what you want the ball to do. Choose which dimple on the ball you want to strike. Swing technique should not be in your conscious thoughts, as this can lead to paralysis by analysis. Stick to one or two key thoughts so you avoid overthinking, and always aim for a small, precise target.

CONCLUSION

Now you know how to make your practice more effective, your challenge really begins. Commit to the process of getting better, and start today.

On the course, focus on what you can control. Always aim at a small, precise target, set a clear intention for each shot and fully commit to it. If any doubts arise, walk away and reset, so you give yourself the best opportunity for each shot to match your intention. Learn to accept the outcome.

Work through the practice section and record your playing statistics so you spend the majority of your time improving the shots that will be the most influential in reducing your scores. Always plan your practice in advance, and set goals for each session which you can achieve if you perform well. If a practice does not challenge you, it will not improve you as much as one that pushes you to or just beyond your current limit, and you will never find out how good you can be. Make your practice measurable and always record your results. Every time you achieve a goal, note it and celebrate your success. Make getting better a fun and enjoyable process!

Build a functional swing that gets the ball where you want it to go. Don't worry how it looks or get too caught up in technique. How you strike the ball is what really matters. There are no score reductions for the prettiest swing. Often, spending time doing training and tournament practices will reduce scores more than working on swing technique.

What you do in practice will influence your progress, and so will your attitude and how you do it. Two people can do exactly the same practice and hit the same number of balls. One person can hit each shot with a clear intention and give every ball their full attention. Another player can go through the motions mindlessly. When this happens, it's not difficult to guess who will make the most progress. If you have the same desire and determination to achieve scores in practice that you have on the course, you will reap the rewards.

Your attitude influences everything you do, so always do your best. Be patient and persistent. The road to improvement is full of highs, lows and plateaus. It will never be a smooth ride, but a good, productive attitude and systematically following and building on the practices and processes in this book will accelerate your progress and help you to play your best golf. Enjoy turning better practice into better golf. Today is your opportunity to start to see just how good you can be!

PART II - LET'S PRACTICE!

All of the practices are broken down into different shot and type of practice sections. Every time you finish one practice, work on a different shot next. You can increase the challenge by practicing two shot types concurrently and alternating between shots or sets of shots, e.g. driving and putting. On the course, you are unlikely to use the same club many times in a row, so by mixing up your practice, you will become more adaptable and better prepared to play golf.

Every practice has a scorecard provided. Once you have completed the practice and filled it in, record your results in a notebook so you have a target score to beat next time. Practice will always be most productive and fun when you are trying to accomplish scores you feel are just within reach if you perform well. Every time you set a new personal best, write it down. Be proud of your progress and celebrate your success!

Some of the practices have target size options based on the sizes of fairways and greens or one- and two-putt distances. Use the generic ones most appropriate to your skill / playing level, or if you already know your average proximities to the target, you can use them instead and aim to reduce them over time. For your practice to be most effective, it must be challenging, so if at any time a practice feels easy, immediately adapt it by reducing the size of the target or increasing the consequence on each shot. If it doesn't challenge you, it will not improve you as much and you will never know how good you can be!

Some of the practices have three levels. When you are regularly achieving new personal bests and feel ready for a harder, more demanding practice, move to the next level. You will notice the higher levels more closely resemble playing golf.

In some of the shot categories, there are a number of different practices. Choose the ones which will be most beneficial to your game. It's more productive to stick to a few practices so that you progressively improve that skill and better your scores than it is to do a lot of different practices sporadically. With any practice, if you tend to progress quickly until you reach a certain distance and then start to struggle, start some of your sessions at that distance so that your practice is more relevant to your needs and you are training at the edge (margin) of your current abilities.

Whenever you practice, always hole (putt) out. In a stroke-play round, you have to do this, so get into the habit of doing it all of the time. Never take holing a short putt for granted. Over the years, many have been missed, and it has cost players hundreds of thousands of dollars and the opportunity to win major championships. Very few golfers are able to compete for similar amounts of money, but always holing out could be the difference in one day winning a club championship or a few extra pounds from your friends.

KNOW YOUR GAME

To achieve lower scores, it's important to know how far you carry the ball with each club. The easiest and most accurate way to do this is by using a launch monitor such as a Trackman. Many PGA professionals have them, and a session on one will give you your average carry distances, proximities to the target and shot dispersions with each club. If you don't have access to a launch monitor, the following steps will help you. Because it is the carry distance and not the total distance that should be measured, it is best to do this with someone so that they can stand near to where each ball will land, see the exact landing spot and then measure it. Just make sure you don't hit them!

Carry Distances

- Choose a club.

- Aim at a target that's out of reach so it acts only as a target line.

- From random positions on fairway-length grass (tee up your driver), hit 10 shots with a full swing.

- Discard any really poor shots by hitting another ball but leave in slight mishits; the 10 shots should represent your average, not your best 10!

- If you hit a perfect shot, note the distance. This will tell you how far your best shot goes, which can be helpful on the course at times.

- To get a more accurate representation of how you would play on the course and what your distances would be, take time between each shot to hole a four-foot putt or play a short chip if a putting green is not nearby.

- Measure the carry distance of each ball and enter it on the scorecard.

- Calculate your average distance.

- Repeat with every club. This can take a number of sessions to complete properly.

- Enter the distances into the shot matrix on page 125.

- With a Trackman launch monitor, the software will give you your carry distances and average without needing any calculations.

Shot Number	1	2	3	4	5	6	7	8	9	10	Total Dist.	Avg Dist.
Club:												
Club:												
Club:												
Club:												
Club:												
Club:												
Club:												
Club:												
Club:												
Club:												
Club:												
Club:												
Club:												

Proximity to the Target (Clubs)

- Choose a club and set a marker at your average carry distance for that club.

- From random positions on fairway-length grass (tee up your driver), hit 10 shots to the target.

- Discard any really poor shots by hitting another ball but leave in slight mishits; the 10 shots should represent your average, not your best 10!

- To get a more accurate representation of what your accuracy will be on the course, take time between each shot to hole a four-foot putt or play a short chip if a putting green is not nearby.

- Enter the distance each ball lands from the target onto the scorecard.

- Calculate your average proximity to the target.

- Enter the distance into the shot matrix on page 125.

- Repeat with every club. This can take a number of sessions to complete properly.

- With a Trackman launch monitor, the software will give you your average proximity to the target without needing any calculations.

- Aim to reduce your averages and improve your accuracy over time.

Shot Number	1	2	3	4	5	6	7	8	9	10	Total Dist.	Avg Dist.
Club:												
Club:												
Club:												
Club:												
Club:												
Club:												
Club:												
Club:												
Club:												
Club:												
Club:												
Club:												
Club:												

Dr Nicky Lumb & Dr Dave Alred MBE

Approach Shots with Wedges

On the course, most shots will not match the exact distance you hit one of your clubs, and you will have to improvise. To give you more options, if you are a right-handed golfer, imagine your left arm relates to a clock face and use it to create four different back swing lengths.

A 7.30 swing would be ¼ of the way back. A 9 o'clock swing would be ½ way back, with your left arm parallel to the ground. A 10.30 swing would be a ¾ swing, and a 12 o'clock swing would be a full swing. If you record your different backswing lengths and play them on a video, you may not be in exactly the clock face positions you feel you are. This doesn't matter; what is important is that you feel you are in these positions, can distinguish between them and can repeat each swing length when you need to.

Once you can do this, work out your average carry distance and proximity to the target with each wedge and swing length. With a consistent rhythm and tempo, this can be effective with bunker shots as well. You can then become more versatile by making small tweaks to your swing. If a pitching wedge 9 o'clock swing goes 100 yards, and a shot is 95 yards, then you can either choke down on the grip by one inch so the ball goes about five yards shorter or make a slightly shorter backswing. If a shot is 105 yards, you can make your backswing a little longer.

Wedge Distances with Different Swings

- Choose a wedge and swing length, e.g. pitching wedge 9 o'clock (½) swing.

- Aim at a target that's out of reach so it acts only as a target line.

- From random positions on fairway-length grass, hit 10 shots to the target using the same swing length.

- For sand shots, play from 10 random positions with good lies.

- Discard any really poor shots by hitting another ball but leave in slight mishits; the 10 shots should represent your average, not your best 10!

- To get a more accurate representation of what your distances will be on the course, take time between each shot to hole a four-foot putt or play a short chip if a putting green is not nearby.

- Measure the carry distance of each ball and enter it on the scorecard.

- Calculate your average distance.

- Repeat with every wedge and swing length. This can take a number of sessions to complete properly.

- Enter the distances into the shot matrix on page 125.

Dr Nicky Lumb & Dr Dave Alred MBE

Shot Number	1	2	3	4	5	6	7	8	9	10	Total Dist.	Avg Dist.
Club: Swing Length:												
Club: Swing Length:												
Club: Swing Length:												
Club: Swing Length:												
Club: Swing Length:												
Club: Swing Length:												
Club: Swing Length:												
Club: Swing Length:												
Club: Swing Length:												
Club: Swing Length:												
Club: Swing Length:												
Club: Swing Length:												
Club: Swing Length:												

Proximity to the Target (Wedges)

- Set a marker at an average swing length distance.

- From random positions on fairway-length grass, hit 10 shots to the target.

- For sand shots, play from 10 random positions with good lies.

- To get a more accurate representation of what your accuracy will be on the course, take time between each shot to hole a four-foot putt or play a short chip if a putting green is not nearby.

- Enter the distance each ball lands from the target onto the scorecard.

- Calculate your average proximity to the target.

- Repeat with every wedge swing length. This can take a number of sessions to complete properly.

- Enter the distance into the shot matrix on page 125.

- Aim to reduce your averages and improve your accuracy over time.

Dr Nicky Lumb & Dr Dave Alred MBE

Shot Number	1	2	3	4	5	6	7	8	9	10	Total Dist.	Avg Dist.
Club: Swing Length:												
Club: Swing Length:												
Club: Swing Length:												
Club: Swing Length:												
Club: Swing Length:												
Club: Swing Length:												
Club: Swing Length:												
Club: Swing Length:												
Club: Swing Length:												
Club: Swing Length:												
Club: Swing Length:												
Club: Swing Length:												
Club: Swing Length:												

Approach Shot Distance Adjustments

Longer shafts and lower lofts make it more challenging to hit iron shots with four different swing lengths, so you may find it is easier to change your hand position on the grip. Gripping down by one inch reduces the carry distance by about five yards, while two inches takes off about ten yards. Ball position also influences carry distance. Moving the ball forward reduces distance, while placing it further back adds distance. Off a tee, the ball carries about five yards further.

Dr Nicky Lumb & Dr Dave Alred MBE

Matrix

Enter your average carry distance with each club at the top of each cell and your average proximity to the target at the bottom, e.g. 9 iron: average distance 130 yards, average proximity to the target 35 feet. Once the matrix is complete, keep it in your pocket for easy access. Laminating it can be helpful for when you play in the rain.

Check your averages regularly and aim to reduce your average proximities over time.

Club	Full Swing
9	130 35

Club	Full Swing		Club	Full Swing		Club	Full Swing

Wedges	¼ Swing	½ Swing	¾ Swing	Full Swing	Sand	Sand

PROCESSES AND ROUTINES

Your processes and routines are the only factors you can control. You cannot control the outcome of a shot or what others do, but you can control what you do. To get the best out of yourself, focus your attention on your own actions and what you can control. You will notice that as your process scores start to increase, your playing scores will start to decrease.

Process Practices

Small, Precise Target

To create the best opportunity to play great golf, it is vital you choose a small, precise target to aim at on every shot. The smaller the target, the smaller the potential miss and the more accurate your shots are likely to be.

- Play 9 or 18 holes.

- On every shot, choose a small, precise target (e.g. a leaf, part of a tree branch or trunk, the flag or a specific part of the hole).

- Describe the target out loud and at all times either look at the target or keep it in your mind's eye.

- Score how small and precise your target was and how well you could see it in your mind's eye out of 10 with 10/10 the optimal score.

- Enter your score after each shot onto the scorecard.

Dr Nicky Lumb & Dr Dave Alred MBE

- At the end of your round, total your scores. To calculate your average score per shot, divide your total process score by the total shots.

- Record your average score and next time aim to beat it. Every time you set a new personal best, write it down. Be proud of your progress and celebrate your success!

Pre-Shot Process Scorecard – Small, Precise Target											
Hole	Par	Hole Score	Target Hole Score	1	2	3	4	5	6	7	8
1											
2											
3											
4											
5											
6											
7											
8											
9											
Total											
Hole	Par	Hole Score	Target Hole Score	1	2	3	4	5	6	7	8
10											
11											
12											
13											
14											
15											
16											
17											
18											
Total											

Set Your Intention

To play your best golf, choose a small, precise target and set a clear intention for every shot. This will make it easier to objectively assess how well the shot matched your intention and how you can make the next one better.

- Play 9 or 18 holes.
- On every shot, decide what you want the ball to do:
    - Choose a small, precise target.
    - Calculate the shot's distance and playing distance.
    - How do you want the ball to fly (curve or straight)?
    - Will the trajectory be normal, high or low?
- Picture the shot in your mind, then execute it.
- Score how well you set your intention out of 10 with 10/10 meaning your intended shot was very clear. Don't be influenced by how well the shot matched your intention.
- Enter your score onto the scorecard.
- At the end of your round, total your scores. To calculate your average score per shot, divide your total process score by the total shots.
- Record your average score and next time aim to be beat it. Every time you set a new personal best, write it down. Be proud of your progress and celebrate your success!

Dr Nicky Lumb & Dr Dave Alred MBE

			Pre-Shot Process Scorecard – Set Your Intention								
Hole	Par	Hole Score	Intention Hole Score	1	2	3	4	5	6	7	8
1											
2											
3											
4											
5											
6											
7											
8											
9											
Total											
Hole	Par	Hole Score	Intention Hole Score	1	2	3	4	5	6	7	8
10											
11											
12											
13											
14											
15											
16											
17											
18											
Total											

Commitment

Before every shot, you must have a clear and simple plan and be fully committed to it. If any doubts or second thoughts enter your mind, always stop, logically re-evaluate the situation and only restart your hitting process once you are happy and can fully commit to the shot you intend to play.

- Play 9 or 18 holes.

- Choose a small, precise target, set a clear intention and go through your pre-shot routine before every shot.

- Score your commitment on each shot out of 10 with 10/10 meaning you were fully committed.

- At the end of your round, total your scores. To calculate your average score per shot, divide your total process score by the total shots.

- Record your average score and next time aim to beat it. Every time you set a new personal best, write it down. Be proud of your progress and celebrate your success!

Dr Nicky Lumb & Dr Dave Alred MBE

Pre-Shot Process Scorecard – Commitment

Hole	Par	Hole Score	Commitment Hole Score	1	2	3	4	5	6	7	8
1											
2											
3											
4											
5											
6											
7											
8											
9											
Total											

Hole	Par	Hole Score	Commitment Hole Score	1	2	3	4	5	6	7	8
10											
11											
12											
13											
14											
15											
16											
17											
18											
Total											

Self-Talk

The way you speak to yourself before, during and after a shot can increase or decrease your confidence and directly influence your attitude and how you feel on your next shot. Always be positive and uplifting and tell yourself what to do and exactly where you want the ball to go. Become a master in confident and productive dialogue.

- Play 9 or 18 holes.

- Focus on your self-talk.

- Score 2 points every time you say something positive, 1 point if you make a neutral comment, and subtract 3 points if you make a negative comment.

- At the end of your round, total your scores. To calculate your average score per shot, divide your total process score by the total shots.

- Record your average score and next time aim to beat it. Every time you set a new personal best, write it down. Be proud of your progress and celebrate your success!

Dr Nicky Lumb & Dr Dave Alred MBE

Pre-Shot Process Scorecard – Self-talk

Hole	Par	Hole Score	Self-talk Hole Score	1	2	3	4	5	6	7	8
1											
2											
3											
4											
5											
6											
7											
8											
9											
Total											

Hole	Par	Hole Score	Self-talk Hole Score	1	2	3	4	5	6	7	8
10											
11											
12											
13											
14											
15											
16											
17											
18											
Total											

Body Language

Your posture and body language can influence how you think, feel and play. If you stand tall with your shoulders back, head up and eyes looking forward you will feel more alert and confident. Think 'be big and powerful' and take up as much space as possible as you walk round the course and prepare to play each shot.

- Play 9 or 18 holes.

- Focus on your body language.

- Score 2 points every time your posture feels 'big and powerful,' and your head is up and your eyes are looking above the flag or towards the top of the tree line. Subtract 3 points if you feel your shoulders are rounded, your head has dropped or you catch your eyes looking at the ground.

- At the end of your round, total your scores. To calculate your average score per shot, divide your total process score by the total shots.

- Record your average score and next time aim to beat it. Every time you set a new personal best, write it down. Be proud of your progress and celebrate your success!

Pre-Shot Process Scorecard – Body Language

Hole	Par	Hole Score	Body Language Hole Score	1	2	3	4	5	6	7	8
1											
2											
3											
4											
5											
6											
7											
8											
9											
Total											

Hole	Par	Hole Score	Body Language Hole Score	1	2	3	4	5	6	7	8
10											
11											
12											
13											
14											
15											
16											
17											
18											
Total											

OFF THE COURSE

PUTTING

Being able to read a green and achieve a good strike that starts the ball on its intended line and controls its speed are the keys to good putting. The first part of this section will develop your technical skills so more putts match your intention. The second part will challenge your skills with training and tournament practices. Putts are divided into three types: short putts (inside 10ft), medium putts (between 10ft and 25ft), and long putts (over 25ft). With every practice, you will achieve a score which you can aim to beat next time.

(For measuring purposes, a putter is about 3ft).

Technical Practices

Face Control

Striking the ball in the middle of the putter face is important for good putting. If a ball is hit towards the toe of the putter, it often rolls to the right. With a heel strike, the ball can roll left. With a central strike, the ball will roll where the putter face is pointing, so let's get it pointing where the ball needs to go!

Through the Gate

This practice promotes a square putter face at impact and a central strike. The gates provide immediate feedback on your club face control and the starting line of the ball.

Equipment: Putter, 4 tees, ball, chalk line, notebook, pen

- Find a straight putt and draw a 5ft chalk line to the hole.

- Impact Gate: 4ft from the hole, place a ball on the line and create a gate with a tee on either side of the chalk line that is just wider than your putter.

- Ball Gate: One foot in front of the ball, create a gate with two tees that is just wider than a ball.

- Line the ball up so that the manufacturer's logo or line on the ball is pointing horizontally along the chalk line.

Level 1

- Achieve 10 straight rolls along the chalk line, through the ball gate and into the hole without hitting any of the tees.

- The logo or line on the ball should roll in a straight line without spinning or skidding.

10 Rolls Through Gate	Achieved	

Level 2

- Achieve 10 consecutive straight rolls along the chalk line, through the ball gate and into the hole without hitting any of the tees.

10 Consecutive Rolls Through Gate	Achieved	

Dr Nicky Lumb & Dr Dave Alred MBE

Aim at a Coin

Aiming at the hole is too big a target. Inside right is different to right edge and right half is different to right centre. The smaller the target, the smaller the potential miss. Aiming at a coin will help you to be more precise with your aim.

Equipment: Putter, coin, 4 balls, notebook, pen

Level 1

- Place a coin on the green.

- Starting at 2ft, how many attempts does it take to roll a ball over the coin 3 times?

- Move 1ft back and repeat from 3ft, then from 4ft and so on.

- How many attempts does it take to roll 3 balls over the coin from each distance?

- Complete the scorecard.

Distance	2ft	3ft	4ft	5ft	6ft	Total
Putts Over Coin	3	3	3	3	3	15
Attempts						

Level 2

- Imagine a clock face and place one ball at 12, 3, 6 and 9 o'clock, two feet from the coin.

- How many putts does it take to roll each ball over the coin and stop it within 1ft?

- Repeat this process from each distance.

Distance	2ft	3ft	4ft	5ft	6ft	Total
Putts Over Coin	4	4	4	4	4	20
Attempts						

Level 3

- From 2ft, how many attempts does it take to roll a ball over the coin from 12, 3, 6 and 9 o'clock in consecutive putts?
- Move 1ft further back and repeat for 3ft, 4ft, etc.

Distance	2ft	3ft	4ft	5ft	6ft	Total
Consecutive Putts Over Coin	4	4	4	4	4	20
Attempts						

- Record your scores and next time aim to complete each distance in one putt less. Every time you set a new personal best, write it down. Be proud of your progress and celebrate your success!

Where Will the Ball Enter the Hole?

If a putt is flat, then assuming a straight roll, the ball should enter the hole at 6 o'clock. If a putt has a right to left slope, then the ball will fall to the left before dropping into the hole at 5 o'clock. With a more severe break, it may fall into the hole at 4 or even 3 o'clock. If a putt breaks from left to right, then the ball will fall to the right and drop into the hole at 7 or 8 o'clock or even 9 o'clock. On faster greens, a ball breaks more, so a downhill putt will break more than an uphill one. A ball also breaks more as it slows down.

Type of Putt	Speed	Break
Flat		No Break
Flat Right to Left		Aim Right
Flat Left to Right		Aim Left
Uphill	Slower Hit Harder	No Break
Uphill Right to Left	Slower Hit Harder	Aim Right
Uphill Left to Right	Slower Hit Harder	Aim Left
Downhill	Faster Hit Softer	No Break
Downhill Right to Left	Faster Hit Softer	Aim Right
Downhill Left to Right	Faster Hit Softer	Aim Left

Deciding where the ball will enter the hole and working backwards from the hole to the ball on the target line can help you to build a feel and a picture in your mind of what the ball will do so you can determine the best start line and speed.

Pace the Distance

Pacing the distance of a putt instead of guessing its length can help you to more effectively judge the distance and speed of every putt. It's essential to know how far you intend to hit an approach shot into a green, and the same rationale on the greens equips your brain with more information which can lead to better accuracy and consistency.

Once you become familiar with the feel for certain distances, you can start to calibrate your feel depending on the speed of a green. A 20ft putt on a fast green may play like an 18ft putt on a green speed you are more used to. On a slower green a 20ft putt may equate to a 22ft putt.

Speed Determines Line, Line Determines Speed

With every breaking putt, there are a variety of speed and line combinations that could hole the ball. Capture speed is the speed at which a ball can fall into the hole. If a ball is travelling too fast as it approaches, then the hole's effective size reduces and it's less likely the ball will drop. If a ball is travelling more slowly, the hole's effective size increases, and the ball is more likely to fall. Most golfers have a preference with their putting speed and read putts accordingly. Some read less break and hit the ball firmly so that the ball hits the back of the hole and dives in. Others see more curve and hit the ball softly so that the break brings the ball into the hole and it drops in on its last roll. Whatever your preference, the key to good putting is having a picture in your mind of how the ball will roll into the hole and matching up your read, line and speed.

3 Tee Bowling

The more a putt breaks, the more start line and speed options you have. This practice will help you to match different lines and speeds and determine where the ball will enter the hole.

Equipment: Putter, 3 tees, 3 balls, notebook, pen

- Choose a 6ft putt with a left to right break.
- Place tees lightly into the ground just in front of the hole at 6, 7 and 8 o'clock.
- Use the same starting position for each putt.
- Putt the first ball so it knocks down the tee at 6 o'clock and drops into the hole.
- Repeat with the tee at 7 o'clock and then 8 o'clock.
- Do this 3 times.
- Note the different speeds and lines needed to knock down each tee and hole the putt.

Tick On Completion	

- Repeat with right to left breaking putts.

Tick On Completion	

Practicing on different greens with varying slopes and undulations will accustom you to line and speed variations.

Halfway Ball Gate

When a putt does not match your intention, it's important to try and work out why. Placing a gate halfway along the intended line of a putt and seeing if the ball goes through it and where it finishes gives immediate feedback on your read, line and speed.

Equipment: Putter, 2 tees, 3 balls, notebook, pen

Level 1

- Select a 4ft putt.
- Choose a target line and at the halfway (2ft) point, create a two-ball-wide gate with tees.
- Roll the ball through the gate and into the hole.
- Change holes after every successful putt.
- Vary the hole distances between 4ft and 6ft.
- How many attempts does it take to roll a ball through a halfway gate and hole 10 different putts?

Distance	4-6ft
Putts Holed With Ball Rolling Through Gate	10
Attempts	

Dr Nicky Lumb & Dr Dave Alred MBE

Level 2

- How many attempts does it take to roll a ball through a halfway gate and hole 10 different putts between 6ft and 10ft?

Distance	6-10ft
Putts Holed With Ball Rolling Through Gate	10
Attempts	

Level 3

- Make the halfway gate 2" wider than the size of your putter from heel to toe.

- How many putts does it take to roll a ball through a halfway gate and hole or have 5 different putts finish within 2ft of the hole between 10ft and 25ft?

Distance	10-25ft
Putts Holed With Ball Rolling Through Gate	5
Attempts	

- Record your scores and next time aim to complete each practice in fewer putts. Every time you set a new personal best, write it down. Be proud of your progress and celebrate your success!

Quantifying Your Stroke

Tempo is the overall speed of your putting stroke. Some players have a quick stroke, while others are much slower. Rhythm is how quickly you take the putter back in relation to the speed you bring it down to impact. Most good putters have a 2:1 ratio, so their backswing takes twice as long as their downswing to impact. This stays the same regardless of the putts length. Counting one, two; one for the backswing, and two from the start of the downswing through to the finish is a good way to maintain rhythm.

With a consistent rhythm and tempo, the length of your backswing can control the distance of your putts. This works in the same way as knowing how far the ball flies with different swing lengths in your long game. By relating the distance of your backswing to how far you feel you take the putter back (4", 8", 12"), you can build quantifiable feels for different distances.

These can then be adapted depending on the speed of the greens and whether putts are uphill or downhill. A downhill 10ft putt on a fast green may equate to a 6ft stroke, while an uphill 10ft putt on a slow green may need a 12ft stroke. By assigning feels to a few stroke lengths, your putting can become more consistent and adaptable over time.

To start with, establish a feel for two or three distances and then build on them.

- Find a flat area on a green.
- Choose a backswing length / reference point (e.g. 4")

Dr Nicky Lumb & Dr Dave Alred MBE

- Putt 10 balls using the same backswing length and tempo.

- Measure the distance of each ball (they should all be at a similar distance).

- Calculate your average distance.

- Repeat this process using other backswing lengths, e.g. 8" and 12"

Before you play, spend a few minutes on the practice green calibrating your backswing lengths with the speed of the greens for that day.

Look for Patterns

Becoming aware of any putting tendencies will accelerate your progress. When putts do not match your intention, note whether the ball finishes left or right of the hole and if your read was straight, left to right or right to left. Did your read match the line?

On longer putts, is your distance control consistent or are putts consistently finishing long or short of the hole? Noting this information will help you to recognise any patterns so you can learn from them and get more putts to match your intention.

Putt with Your Eyes Closed

Putting with your eyes closed, predicting the outcome and then opening your eyes to see the result will sharpen your ability to feel a putt and develop your distance control.

Dr Nicky Lumb & Dr Dave Alred MBE

Training Practices

The following training practices will help you to develop all of your putting skills. To move any practice closer to a tournament practice, play a chip or hit a full shot before a putt or set of putts so your practice more closely represents what you do on the course.

Speed Control Lag Putting

As a putt gets longer, the likelihood of holing it reduces. From longer distances, aim to get the ball to finish as close to the hole as possible so you are more likely to hole the next one. If the first putt goes in, it's a bonus. A PGA Tour player holes an average of five putts over 10 feet per event. Over 20 feet, this drops to less than 1.5 putts, so it's important to be a good lag putter!

Equipment: Putter, 4 tees, 3 balls, notebook, pen

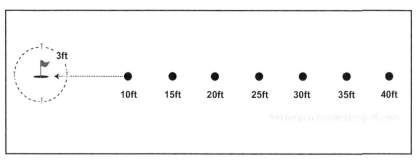

Figure 12. Speed Control Lag Putting Practice

Level 1

- Place tees 3ft from the hole at 12, 3, 6 and 9 o'clock.

- How many putts does it take to get 3 balls inside 3ft from 10ft?

- Once you have achieved this, move 5ft back and repeat from 15ft, 20ft, 25ft, 30ft, 35ft and 40ft.

- Complete the scorecard.

Distance	10ft	15ft	20ft	25ft	30ft	35ft	40ft
Putts Finishing Inside 3ft	3	3	3	3	3	3	3
Attempts							

Level 2

- How many attempts does it take to get 3 consecutive putts inside 3ft from each distance?

- Change holes or direction after completing each distance.

Distance	10ft	15ft	20ft	25ft	30ft	35ft	40ft
Consecutive Putts Finishing Inside 3ft	3	3	3	3	3	3	3
Attempts							

Dr Nicky Lumb & Dr Dave Alred MBE

Level 3

- Working your way around a green, how many putts does it take to get each first putt within 3ft of the hole and then hole your second putt at each distance?

- If your first putt finishes outside 3ft or you miss the second putt, add the putts to your score and then go back and replay the hole. Keep playing until you successfully complete the requirements at all 7 distances.

Distance	10ft	15ft	20ft	25ft	30ft	35ft	40ft
Score							

- Record your scores and next time aim to complete each practice in fewer putts. Every time you set a new personal best, write it down. Be proud of your progress and celebrate your success!

- With any of the levels, if you regularly reach a distance you start to struggle at, adapt the practice and start your next session 5 feet inside that distance and then continue so you are focusing on your weaker distances and making the practice more relevant and challenging.

Up and Down the Ladder

Good speed and distance control will create more opportunities to hole putts and make three putting less likely.

Equipment: Putter, balls, coin, notebook, pen

Up the Ladder

- Roll your first putt to a coin at 10ft.

- Aim to get your next putt slightly further.

- The goal is to get each ball to finish just past the previous one. If a ball finishes short, level with it or more than 3ft past the previous ball, that round is over.

- To improve your feel, as soon as you have hit each ball, predict where the ball will finish in relation to the previous putt.

- Record your score, which is the distance the furthest ball travels and the number of consecutive putts that score within that space.

Down the Ladder

- Starting at 30ft, or if it is further the distance you reached on the Up the Ladder round, do the reverse, aiming to get each ball to stop a little closer to the coin at 10ft.

- Record your score.

- Repeat both exercises 3 times.

- Record your best score in each direction and next time aim to get one more ball inside the space. Every time you set a new personal best, write it down. Be proud of your progress and celebrate your success!

Attempt Distance / Number of Balls	1	2	3	Total
Up the Ladder Score				
Down the Ladder Score				

- This practice can be adapted to improve your speed control at any distance. If you struggle on putts over 20ft, start the practice at 20ft and see how many balls you can get between 20ft and 30ft, making sure each ball goes just past the previous one. Then work in reverse from 30ft to 20ft.

- With shorter distances, this practice works well on an indoor carpet.

Tournament Practices

Every putt in this section is unique. To turn any practice into a more challenging tournament practice, play a chip, hit a full shot or walk to the side of the putting green and make a full shot practice swing before every putt so that you are replicating what you do before most putts on the course.

Your One-Putt Distance

Your one-putt range is the distance you need longer putts and chip shots to finish inside to give you the best chance of holing out. It can help you to be realistic with your shot expectations. If your one-putt distance is 3ft, don't beat yourself up if you miss a 6ft putt. If you hole it, it's a bonus!

Equipment: Putter, ball, notebook, pen

- Place a ball 1ft from the hole at 12 o'clock.
- If you hole it, place the ball 1ft from the hole at 6 o'clock.
- If you hole it, repeat from 3 o'clock and then 9 o'clock.
- When you have holed all 4 putts in a row, move 1ft further back and repeat.
- If you miss a putt, go back to the beginning and start again.
- How far back can you go?
- Record your score and next time aim to get one foot further back. Every time you set a new personal best, write it down. Be proud of your progress and celebrate your success!

One-putt Distance	

Dr Nicky Lumb & Dr Dave Alred MBE

Your Two-Putt Distance

Your two-putt range is the distance from which you can consistently get longer putts to finish inside your one-putt distance. For this practice, lets assume it's three feet. The longer it is, the more two putts you will make. This can help you to be realistic with your expectations. If your two-putt distance is 18 feet, and a 30-foot putt doesn't finish inside three feet, don't tell yourself off! Based on your current skill level, getting the ball inside three feet with your first putt would be a bonus.

Equipment: Putter, ball, notebook, pen

- Choose a hole and make a 10ft putt. Aim to get the ball to finish as near to the hole as possible. The putt counts as a score if it finishes inside 3ft. You can mark this out with tees 3ft from the hole at 12, 3, 6 and 9 o'clock or use the length of your putter (usually about 3ft) to determine each putt's accuracy.

- Repeat this process from 2 different positions 10ft from a hole.

- If both putts finish inside 3ft, move 2ft further back and repeat the process.

- If any ball finishes outside 3ft, go back to the beginning and start again.

- How far back can you go?

- Record your score and next time aim to get two feet further back. Every time you set a new personal best, write it down. Be proud of your progress and celebrate your success!

Two-putt Distance	

Short Putts Inside 10ft

3-5ft

Equipment: Putter, ball, 12 tees, notebook, pen

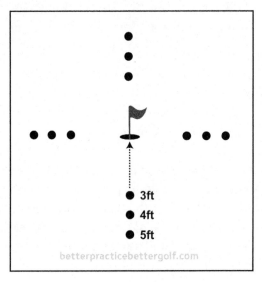

Figure 13. 3-5ft Putting Practice

Level 1

- Use tees to mark 12, 3, 6 and 9 o'clock at 3ft, 4ft, and 5ft from a hole.

- Go through your pre-putt routine before every putt.

- How many putts does it take to hole all 12 putts?

- If you miss any 3ft putts, start again.

Distance	3ft	4ft	5ft	Total
Putts Holed	4	4	4	12
Number of Putts				

Dr Nicky Lumb & Dr Dave Alred MBE

Level 2

- How many putts does it take to hole all 12 putts?
- If you miss any 3ft or 4ft putts, start again.

Distance	3ft	4ft	5ft	Total
Putts Holed	4	4	4	12
Number of Putts				

Level 3

- How many putts does it take to hole all 12 putts consecutively?
- If you miss any putt, start again.

Distance	3ft	4ft	5ft	Total
Putts Holed	4	4	4	12
Number of Putts				

- Record your scores and next time aim to complete each practice in fewer putts. Every time you set a new personal best, write it down. Be proud of your progress and celebrate your success!

5-10ft

Equipment: Putter, 6 tees, ball, notebook, pen

Level 1

- Place tees randomly around a hole at 5ft, 6ft, 7ft, 8ft, 9ft and 10ft.
- Go through your pre-putt routine on every putt.

- Putt in a random order.

- When you hole a putt, push the tee into the ground. If you miss a putt, move to a different putt next unless it is the last one.

- When you have holed all 6 putts on one hole, repeat on a different hole.

- How many putts does it take to hole all 12 putts?

Distance	Putts Holed	Number of Putts
5-10ft	12	

Level 2

- How many putts does it take to hole all 12 putts?
- If you miss either 5ft putt, start again.

Distance	Putts Holed	Number of Putts
5-10ft	12	

Level 3

- How many putts does it take to hole all 12 putts?
- If you miss any 5ft or 6ft putts, start again.

Distance	Putts Holed	Number of Putts
5-10ft	12	

- Record your scores and next time aim to complete each practice in fewer putts. Every time you set a new personal best, write it down. Be proud of your progress and celebrate your success!

Dr Nicky Lumb & Dr Dave Alred MBE

3-10ft

Equipment: Putter, 9 tees, ball, notebook, pen, wedge for Level 2

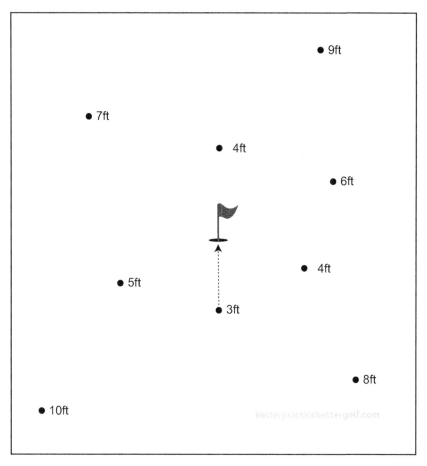

Figure 14. 3-10ft Putting Practice

Level 1

- Place tees randomly around a hole at 3ft, 4ft x 2, 5ft, 6ft, 7ft, 8ft, 9ft, 10ft.

- Go through your pre-putt routine on every putt.

- Putt in a random order.

- When you hole a putt, push the tee into the ground. If you miss a putt, place the tee on its side.

- When you have completed one hole, repeat on a different hole.

- Score the following: 1 putt = -1, 2 putts = 0, 3 putts = +1, leave any putt short = +1.

- With 18 putts, how low can you go?

Distance	Number of Putts	Score
3-10ft	18	

Level 2

- Repeat Level 1 while playing a chip shot within 20 yards before every putt. If a green you can chip on is not nearby, make a full shot practice swing on the edge of the green before every putt.

- Based on your skill level, score how many chips finish inside 3ft or 6ft.

- Over 18 putts, how low can you go?

Distance	Number of Putts	Score
3-10ft	18	

Chip Shots Inside 20yds	Chips Finishing Inside 3ft / 6ft
18	

- Record your scores and next time aim to be one shot better. Every time you set a new personal best, write it down. Be proud of your progress and celebrate your success!

Dr Nicky Lumb & Dr Dave Alred MBE

Medium Putts 10-25ft

Equipment: Putter, 3 balls, notebook, pen

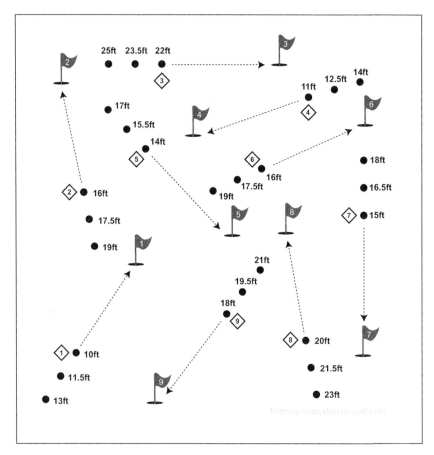

Figure 15. 10-25ft Putting Practice

- Choose a hole 10ft to 22ft away and drop a ball.

- Drop 2 balls on the same line with each ball 1.5ft further back.

- Go through your pre-shot routine on each putt.

- If any ball finishes short of the hole, move it one putter length back and play on.

- Always hole out.

- Play to a different hole each time.

- Score the following: 1 putt = -1, 2 putts = 0, 3 putts = +1, 4 putts = +2.

- Over 9 holes, how low can you go?

- To introduce pressure, set a target score. If you do not reach it, give yourself one opportunity to hole a 6ft putt, with a consequence of repeating the practice or choosing an unwelcome penalty.

- Record your scores and next time aim to be one shot better. Every time you set a new personal best, write it down. Be proud of your progress and celebrate your success!

Distance	Number of Holes Played	Score
10-25ft	9	

Long Putts Over 25ft

Equipment: Putter, 3 balls, notebook, pen

Level 1

- Choose a hole over 25ft away and randomly drop a ball.

- Drop 2 balls on the same line with each ball 2ft further back.

- Go through your pre-putt routine on each putt.

- Always hole out.

- Play to a different hole each time and incorporate the longest holes on the green.

- Score the following: 1 putt = -1, 2 putts = 0, 3 putts = +1, 4 putts = +2.

- Over 9 holes, how low can you go?

Distance	Number of Holes Played	Score
Over 25ft	9	

Level 2

- Use the same method as Level 1.

- If any putt finishes outside 3ft, move that ball one putter length back and play on.

Distance	Number of Holes Played	Score
Over 25ft	9	

- Record your scores and next time aim to be one putt better. Every time you set a new personal best, write it down. Be proud of your progress and celebrate your success!

SHORT GAME

Short game practice involves all shots off the green inside 50 yards. Every practice can be broken into 10-yard yardage bands, such as 10-20 yards, or bands can be combined. On the course, most short game shots are played within 20 yards, so the practices focus on this range. If there is a distance you play from more often, adapt the practice so it better suits your needs.

On the course, short game shots vary in difficulty. Some shots will be straight forward from good fairway lies with plenty of green to work with. Other shots will be from poor lies with carries over water or sand with little green to work with. Every practice starts with good lies in the fairway or sand, so you can focus on achieving a good strike. As you progress, vary your lies so that you practice from the rough and awkward lies as well. Your practice should represent the full variety of shots you will face on the course.

Before you play any shot, choose a precise landing spot. See in your mind exactly what you want the ball to do from the moment it comes off your club face to where and how it lands and reaches the hole. Be attentive to where and how every ball lands in relation to your intention, so you can learn from every shot you hit.

Dr Nicky Lumb & Dr Dave Alred MBE

Technical Practices

With short game shots, we often have to be creative and change the trajectory and height so that some shots fly higher and others lower. Sometimes you will need the ball to stop quickly; on other occasions, you will want more roll. You can do this by using clubs with more loft for higher shots and less loft for lower ones.

Moving the ball forwards in your stance will shallow your attack angle, increase the amount of loft delivered to the ball and engage more bounce (angle between the leading edge and trailing edge of the club head), making the ball fly higher. Moving the ball position backwards has the opposite effect. It steepens the angle of attack, reduces the amount of loft delivered, engages more of the leading edge and uses less bounce so that the ball flies lower and runs more. Opening the club face also influences the ball's flight, roll and spin. Some shots will need just one of these interventions, while others will require more.

For standard short game shots, a good strike is usually achieved when the club face strikes the ball just before it lightly brushes the ground. This makes impact a slight downward strike, with the lowest point of the swing just after the club face has hit the ball. It's important that the club head doesn't dig into the ground, so try to feel the club 'surf the turf.' Using the bounce can help you as it increases forgiveness so you get better results from less than perfect strikes.

Many golfers play most of their shots around the green with one or two wedges so they can build strong feels. If you often use more than one club to play a shot, change clubs at any time and mark this on the scorecard. By recording your scores, you will know which wedge is most accurate. It is also beneficial to practice with other clubs at times so that you become more adaptable and can call upon an array of shot options.

Where Are You Now?

The purpose of practice is to improve your skills and shoot lower scores on the course. To do this, you need to know where you are now so that you always have scores to beat and can measure and monitor your progress over time and improve your game through practice.

Proximity to the Hole

- Choose a hole within 10 yards.

- If more than one hole is available, use 2 or 3.

- From different fairway positions inside 10 yards, play 10 chip shots to the target(s).

- To get a more accurate representation of what your accuracy will be on the course, hole a four-foot putt between each shot.

- For every shot, use the club you feel will give you the best result, or if you usually use more than one wedge around the greens, repeat this practice using a second wedge so you can compare their accuracy.

- Measure the distance each ball finishes from its target.

- Fill in the scorecard.

- Calculate your average score.

- Repeat from 10-20 yards, 20-30 yards, 30-40 yards and 40-50 yards. This can take a number of sessions to complete properly.

- Repeat inside 20 yards from good sand lies in the bunker.

- Record your scores.

- Repeat this practice every month and aim to reduce your averages and improve your accuracy over time.

Distance from the Hole	1	2	3	4	5	6	7	8	9	10	Total Dist.	Avg
< 10 Yards Club:												
< 10 Yards Club:												
10-20 Yards Club:												
10-20 Yards Club:												
20-30 Yards Club:												
20-30 Yards Club:												
30-40 Yards Club:												
30-40 Yards Club:												
40-50 Yards Club:												
40-50 Yards Club:												
Sand < 20 Yards Club:												
Sand < 20 Yards Club:												

Training Practices

The following training practices will help you to develop your short game skills. To move any practice closer to a tournament practice, hit a full shot before a short game shot so your practice more closely represents what you do on the course.

Landing Spots

Being able to land a ball on an intended spot will develop your striking consistency, and knowing how it is likely to react on landing and how much it is likely to roll is important for good chipping. With a 60-degree wedge, the ball will usually fly higher and stop quickly. With a pitching wedge, which has less loft, the ball will fly much lower and run more.

Equipment: Wedges, 3 balls, 4 or 5 tees, coin or scorecard, notebook, pen

- Place a coin on a green 5 yards from the edge. If you struggle to see a coin, use a scorecard and secure it with a tee.

- Put tees at 12, 3, 6 and 9 o'clock 3ft around the coin. Based on your skill level, from 20 yards or more, place the tees 6ft from the coin if you need to. (For measuring purposes, a wedge is about 3ft).

- From different fairway positions at 5 yards, hit 3 balls. Aim to land each ball on the coin.

- Before every shot, visualise the ball landing on the coin.

- How many shots does it take to land 3 balls inside the marked area?

- Record your scores.

- Note how far each ball rolls once it has landed. This will help you determine where shots need to land to reach targets in the future.

- Repeat from 10, 15, 20, 30 and 40 yards.

- If you usually use more than one wedge, repeat this practice using the clubs you would often use so you can compare their accuracy.

- Record your scores and next time aim to land 3 balls in each scoring zone in one shot less. Every time you set a new personal best, write it down. Be proud of your progress and celebrate your success!

- If you start at 6ft from 20 yards, aim to gradually reduce the size of the scoring zone over time.

Distance	5yds	10yds	15yds	20yds	30yds	40yds
Scoring Zone Size	3ft	3ft	3ft	3ft / 6ft	3ft / 6ft	3ft / 6 ft
Club: No. of Shots:						
Club: No. of Shots:						
Club: No. of Shots:						

Dr Nicky Lumb & Dr Dave Alred MBE

Landing Spots – How Far Can You Go?

Equipment: Wedges, 3 balls, 4 or 5 tees, coin or scorecard, notebook, pen

Level 1

- Place a coin on a green 5 yards from the edge (use a scorecard if a coin is too small to see).

- Put tees at 12, 3, 6 and 9 o'clock 3ft around the coin.

- Hit 3 balls from fairway grass.

- When you have landed 3 balls in the marked area, hole one four-foot putt, then move three yards back and repeat from 8 yards.

- Always hole one four-foot putt before moving three yards further back.

- Set a time limit, e.g. 15 minutes. How far back can you go?

Time	Distance

Level 2

- Place a coin on a green 5 yards from the edge.

- Put tees at 12, 3, 6 and 9 o'clock 3ft around the coin.

- Every time you land 3 consecutive shots in the marked area, attempt to hole one four-foot putt. If you hole it, move three yards further back and repeat from 8 yards. If you miss the putt, go back to the distance you just chipped from.

- Set a time limit, e.g. 15 minutes. How far back can you go?

Time	Distance

- Record your scores and next time aim to get three yards further back. Every time you set a new personal best, write it down. Be proud of your progress and celebrate your success!

- If you consistently reach a certain distance such as 14 yards and struggle to get further back, adapt the practice and start your next session at 11 yards so you are always working at the edge of your current ability.

Dr Nicky Lumb & Dr Dave Alred MBE

Chip and Runs – How Far Can You Go?

Your next shot will always be played where your ball finishes, so it's important to get the ball to finish as close to the target as possible.

Equipment: Wedges, 3 balls, putter, notebook, pen

Level 1

- Choose a hole 10 yards from the edge of the green.

- Put tees at 12, 3, 6 and 9 o'clock 3ft around the hole.

- Scatter 3 balls on fairway grass.

- Play every ball as it lies.

- When 3 balls finish inside the marked area, hole one four-foot putt, then move three yards back and repeat from 13 yards.

- Always hole one four-foot putt before moving three yards further back.

- Set a time limit, e.g. 15 minutes. How far back can you go?

Time	Distance

Level 2

- Use Level 1's method.

- Every time 3 consecutive shots finish inside the marked area, attempt to hole one four-foot putt. If you hole it, move three yards further back and repeat from 13 yards. If you miss the putt, go back to the distance you just chipped from.

- Set a time limit, e.g. 15 minutes. How far back can you go?

Time	Distance

- Record your scores and next time aim to get three yards further back. Every time you set a new personal best, write it down. Be proud of your progress and celebrate your success!

- If you consistently reach a certain distance such as 19 yards and struggle to get further back, adapt the practice and start your next session at 16 yards so you are always working at the edge of your current ability.

Dr Nicky Lumb & Dr Dave Alred MBE

Achieve 9 Chips in the Scoring Zone

Equipment: Wedges, 3 balls, notebook, pen

- Choose a hole between 10 and 20 yards. If more than one hole is available, use two or three.

- Scatter 3 balls on fairway grass.

- Play every ball as it lies.

- Before every shot, choose a precise landing spot. If you struggle to visualise one, decide where you want the ball to land and place a coin on that spot so you have a target to aim at.

- Move around the green and alternate between holes.

- Based on your skill level, choose a scoring zone of 3ft, 6ft or your average proximity to the hole. The target size should be challenging but achievable.

- How many shots does it take to achieve 9 shots inside the scoring zone?

- Record your scores and next time aim to complete the practice in one shot less. Every time you set a new personal best, write it down. Be proud of your progress and celebrate your success!

- Aim to gradually reduce the size of the scoring zone over time.

Scoring Zone Size:	1	2	3	4	5	6	7	8	9	Total
Attempts										

Jumping Up and Running Down the Ladder

This practice will develop your ability to land a ball on your intended spot as well as your distance control.

Equipment: Wedges, 5 balls, notebook, pen

Jumping Up the Ladder

- Use a flag or marker at 30 yards as your aim line.

- Place a marker in line with the flag at 5 yards.

- Hit from fairway grass.

- Hit the first ball to the 5-yard marker.

- The goal is to get each ball to land just past the previous one.

- If any ball lands short or level with the previous ball, that round is over.

- Your Jumping Up the Ladder score is the number of consecutive shots you can get in between 5 and 30 yards before any ball travels less distance than the previous shot.

- Record your score.

Running Down the Ladder

- Hit the first shot to the flag at 30 yards.

- The goal is to get each ball to finish just short of the previous one.

- If any ball passes or finishes level with the previous ball, that round is over.

Dr Nicky Lumb & Dr Dave Alred MBE

- Your score is the number of consecutive shots you hit between 30 and 5 yards before any ball travels further than the previous one.

- Repeat both exercises 3 times.

- Record your best score and next time aim to get one more ball inside the space. Every time you set a new personal best, write it down. Be proud of your progress and celebrate your success!

Attempt	*1*	*2*	*3*	*Total*
Jumping Up the Ladder Score				
Running Down the Ladder Score				

Sand Landing Spots

Equipment: Wedges, 3 balls, 4 tees, notebook, pen

- Choose a hole within 10 yards of a bunker.

- Based on your skill level, put tees at 12, 3, 6 and 9 o'clock 6ft, 10ft or your average proximity around the hole.

- Use 3 balls.

- From different positions in the bunker, aim to land each ball in the hole.

- Before every shot, visualise the ball landing in the hole.

- How many shots does it take to land 3 balls inside the marked area?

- Record your scores.

- Note how far each ball rolls once it has landed. This will help you determine where shots need to land to reach targets in the future.

- Repeat between 10-20 yards and 20-30 yards.

- Record your scores and next time aim to land 3 balls in each scoring zone in one shot less. Every time you set a new personal best, write it down. Be proud of your progress and celebrate your success!

- Aim to gradually reduce the size of the scoring zone over time.

Distance	Inside 10yds	10-20yds	20-30yds
Scoring Zone Size			
No. of Shots			

Dr Nicky Lumb & Dr Dave Alred MBE

Achieve 9 Sand Shots in the Scoring Zone

Equipment: Wedges, 5 balls, notebook, pen

- Choose a hole within 20 yards. If more than one hole is available, use two or three.

- Scatter 5 balls and use good lies.

- Before every shot, choose a precise landing spot. If you struggle to visualise one, decide where you want the ball to land and place a coin or scorecard on that spot so you have a target to aim at.

- Alternate between holes if it is possible.

- Based on your skill level, choose a scoring zone of 6ft, 10ft or your average proximity to the hole. The target size should be challenging but achievable.

- How many shots does it take to achieve 9 shots inside the scoring zone?

- Record your scores and next time aim to complete the practice in one shot less. Every time you set a new personal best, write it down. Be proud of your progress and celebrate your success!

- Aim to gradually reduce the size of the scoring zone over time.

Scoring Zone Size:	1	2	3	4	5	6	7	8	9	Total
Attempts										

Tournament Practices

Every shot in this section is unique. To turn any practice into a more challenging tournament practice, hit a full shot or make a full shot practice swing before playing every chip shot so that you replicate what you do before every short game shot on the course.

How Many Shots to Achieve 9 Up and Downs?

Equipment: Wedges, ball, putter, notebook, pen

- Use one ball.
- Each hole is a par 2, 10 to 20 yards long.
- Move around the green and use different flags.
- Include fairway, semi-rough, rough and sand lies.
- Include different slopes and lies (uphill and downhill lies, ball above and below feet).
- Always choose a small, precise landing spot, and picture how you want the ball to reach the hole. If you struggle to visualise a landing spot, chose one and place a coin on it so you have a target to aim at.
- Before every shot, go through your pre-shot routine.
- Always hole out.
- How many holes does it take to achieve 9 up and downs?
- Put yourself under pressure by setting a target for the number of holes you have to complete the practice. If it takes more, give yourself one opportunity to get up and

Dr Nicky Lumb & Dr Dave Alred MBE

down from 20-yards, with a consequence of repeating the practice or choosing an unwelcome penalty.

- Record your score and next time aim to complete the practice in one shot less. Every time you set a new personal best, write it down. Be proud of your progress and celebrate your success!

Holes	1	2	3	4	5	6	7	8	9	Total
Attempts										

Par 18

The goal of Par 18 is to get up and down in as few shots as possible.

Equipment: Wedges, ball, putter, notebook, pen

Level 1

- With 1 ball, play 9 holes.
- Each hole is a par 2, 10 to 30 yards long.
- Throw each ball to a random spot on fairway grass and play it as it lies.
- Move around the green and use different flags.
- Include different slopes and lies (uphill and downhill lies, ball above and below feet).
- Always choose a small, precise landing spot, and picture how you want the ball to reach the hole. If you struggle to visualise a landing spot, chose one and place a coin on it so you have a target to aim at.
- Before every shot, go through your pre-shot routine.
- Always hole out.
- Score the following points: 1 shot = -1, 2 shots = 0, 3 shots = +1, 4 shots = +2.

Holes	1	2	3	4	5	6	7	8	9	Total
Score										

Dr Nicky Lumb & Dr Dave Alred MBE

Level 2

- Repeat Level 1 but play 4 shots from fairway grass, 3 shots from the rough and 2 shots from sand.

- Alternate shots between fairway lies.

- To introduce pressure, set a target score. If you do not achieve it, give yourself one opportunity to get up and down from 15yds, with a consequence of repeating the practice or choosing an unwelcome penalty.

Holes	1	2	3	4	5	6	7	8	9	Total
Score										

- Record your scores and next time aim to complete the practice in one shot less. Every time you set a new personal best, write it down. Be proud of your progress and celebrate your success!

LONG GAME

Technical Practices

A perfect strike can create a perfect shot, but a swing that looks perfect will not necessarily produce a perfect strike. Ball striking is the single biggest differentiator between playing standards. The nearer to the middle of the club face you consistently strike a ball, the better golfer you will become. A central strike means more distance, improved control and better accuracy. It feels great too!

Face Strike Control

A ball flies further and straighter when it is hit in the middle of the club face because all of the club's energy goes into it. On a mishit, energy escapes, and many off-line shots are caused by heel or toe strikes. Variable practice encourages you to hit the ball out of the middle, heel and toe of a club so you can differentiate between the movements that create them. This should help you to achieve a central strike more often.

Equipment: Short iron, balls, Dr Scholl's or Daktarin foot spray, notebook, pen

Part 1

- Choose a short iron.

- Spray Dr Scholl's or Daktarin foot spray onto the club face so it's covered with a white film.

- Hit 10 balls.

- Each ball's imprint will show where on the club face you struck the ball and display your strike pattern.

Part 2

- Divide the club face into 3 sections: middle, heel and toe.

- Hit 3 balls out of the toe.

- Hit 3 balls out of the heel.

- Hit 3 balls out of the middle.

- After every shot, based on your feel, predict where the club face hit the ball and then check the impact location.

Toe Strike	1	2	3	Heel Strike	1	2	3	Central Strike	1	2	3
Achieved				Achieved				Achieved			

Part 3

- How many shots does it take to achieve 5 central strikes?

- Change clubs after every shot.

- After every shot, based on your feel, predict where the club face hit the ball and then check the impact location.

- Record your score and next time aim to achieve 5 central strikes in fewer shots.

- Every time you set a new personal best, write it down. Be proud of your progress and celebrate your success!

Central Strikes	1	2	3	4	5	Total
Attempts						

Starting Direction

The direction a club face is pointing in at impact influences the ball's starting direction by up to 75% with an iron and 80% with a driver, so the club face needs to be pointing in the direction you want the ball to start. Being able to hit a ball through a gate will improve your club face control and help to start the ball on its intended line.

Equipment: Short or mid-iron, balls, 4 alignment rods, notebook, pen

Part 1

- Choose a target line and place an alignment rod 2½ feet on either side of it to create a gate 5 yards in front of you. Place two more alignment rods 5 feet from the outer sides of the two rods to create a total of 3 gates.

- Using a short or mid-iron:
  - Hit 5 shots through the left gate.
  - Hit 5 shots through the right gate.
  - Hit 5 shots through the middle.

Shot Achieved	1	2	3	4	5
Left Gate					
Right Gate					
Middle Gate					

Part 2

- Place the alignment rods 3ft apart.
- Hit one ball through the left gate.
- Hit one ball through the right gate.
- Hit one ball through the middle gate.
- Change clubs every 3 shots.
- How many attempts does it take to hit 5 balls through each gate?
- Record your scores and next time aim to complete the gate drill in fewer shots.
- Every time you set a new personal best, write it down. Be proud of your progress and celebrate your success!

Shots Achieved	Left Gate	Right Gate	Middle Gate
1			
2			
3			
4			
5			

Part 3

- Place the alignment rods 3ft apart.

- Hit one ball through the left gate.

- Hit one ball through the right gate.

- Hit one ball through the middle gate.

- Change clubs after every shot.

- How many attempts does it take to hit 10 consecutive balls through the appropriate gate?

- If any ball does not go through the intended gate, restart from zero.

- Record your score and next time aim to complete the gate drill in fewer attempts.

- Every time you set a new personal best, write it down. Be proud of your progress and celebrate your success!

10 Shot Sequence	Attempts	

Ground Contact

Irons – Hitting Down

To achieve a solid iron strike, the lowest point of your swing should be just after you have hit the ball so that all of the club's energy goes into the ball.

Equipment: Short or mid-iron, balls, tees, notebook, pen

- Place a ball on the ground.

- Place a thin towel about 6" behind the ball. Make sure it is far enough back so that your club does not catch it during your backswing.

- Place a tee flat on the ground 2" in front of the ball.

- Hit the ball without touching the towel and brush the grass or take a small shallow divot after the ball so that the tee flies into the air.

- How many shots does it take to achieve 10 solid low point strikes?

- Record your score and next time aim to achieve 10 solid strikes in fewer attempts.

- Every time you set a new personal best, write it down. Be proud of your progress and celebrate your success!

Low Point	1	2	3	4	5	6	7	8	9	10	Total
Attempts											

Driver -- Hitting Up

To hit the ball as far as possible, you need to hit up on the ball and achieve a positive attack angle so the ball has a high launch.

Equipment: Driver, balls, tees, notebook, pen

- Tee up a ball.
- Place a second ball on the ground 4" in front of it on the target line.
- Tilt your body at address so that your right shoulder is below your left shoulder.
- Hit the ball off the tee without touching the second ball.
- How many shots does it take to achieve 10 strikes without hitting the second ball?
- Record your score and next time aim to achieve 10 upward strikes in fewer attempts.
- Every time you set a new personal best, write it down. Be proud of your progress and celebrate your success!

Hitting Up	1	2	3	4	5	6	7	8	9	10	Total
Attempts											

Dr Nicky Lumb & Dr Dave Alred MBE

Curve Control

Swing path is the direction the club head is moving in at impact. Its relationship with the direction the club face is pointing in at impact determines how much the ball will curve during its flight. When the club face and swing path are pointing in the same direction at impact, the ball will fly in a straight line with no curve. The bigger the difference between them, the more the ball will curve, so to reduce curvature, the club face and swing path need to be closer together. There are three path types: in to out, out to in and in to square to in.

Equipment: Mid-iron, balls, head cover, 2 alignment rods, notebook, pen

Part 1

- To build awareness and improve your ability to control the ball's curve:
  - Hit 3 balls that start left of the target and curve to the right (slice).
  - Hit 3 balls that start right of the target and curve left (hook).
  - Hit 3 balls relatively straight.
- You will probably find it easy to hit one of these shapes and much harder to hit the other two.

Slice Out to In Path				Hook In to Out Path				Straight In to Square to In			
Open Club Face	1	2	3	Closed Club Face	1	2	3	Square Club Face	1	2	3
Achieved				Achieved				Achieved			

Part 2

Straighter Shots

- Place a ball on the ground and address it with a short or mid-iron.

- With the club face behind the ball, place a head cover an inch from the toe of the club so that the middle of the head cover is in line with the ball. Over time, move the head cover nearer to the toe so eventually there is hardly any gap.

- Hit a ball without hitting the head cover.

- For more club control, start by making half-swings in slow motion and gradually build up to a full swing before increasing your speed.

- Repeat for 5 shots, then change clubs.

- How many attempts does it take to hit 10 shots that avoid the head cover?

- Record your score and next time aim to achieve 10 hits that avoid the head cover in fewer shots.

- Every time you set a new personal best, write it down. Be proud of your progress and celebrate your success!

Dr Nicky Lumb & Dr Dave Alred MBE

Reducing a Slice

A slice is a left to right ball flight for a right-handed golfer which occurs when the club face is open and the club path moves from 'out to in' through impact. A slicer would usually hit the head cover before the ball by cutting across the ball from right to left. By hitting the ball and avoiding the head cover, the club head will approach the ball from the inside, creating more of an in to square to in path and a straighter ball flight.

Reducing a Hook

A hook is a right to left ball flight which occurs when the club face is closed and the club path moves from 'in to out' through impact. A hooker would usually hit the head cover just after striking the ball. By hitting the ball and avoiding the head cover, a straighter ball flight will be achieved through a more 'in to square to in' swing path.

An in to out swing path can also be neutralized by positioning a head cover on the other side of the ball, so that the middle of it is 1" from the heel of the club. By hitting the ball and avoiding the head cover, the club head will approach the ball from a more neutral position creating a straighter path and ball flight.

To hit straighter shots and further reduce curvature, the club face will need to be neutralized so that the club face and swing path are closer together.

Avoiding the Head Cover	1	2	3	4	5	6	7	8	9	10	Total
Attempts											

Part 3

- Choose a target line and place an alignment rod 1½ feet on either side of it to create a gate 5 yards in front of you.

- Choose a club and hit a ball through the gate without touching the head cover.

- Change clubs.

- How many attempts does it take to hit 10 consecutive shots through the gate without touching the head cover?

- If you hit the head cover or the ball does not go through the gate, start again.

- Record your score and next time aim to achieve 10 consecutive shots in fewer attempts.

- Every time you set a new personal best, write it down. Be proud of your progress and celebrate your success!

10 Consecutive Shots Sequence	Attempts	

Balance

Good balance is one of the keys to good ball striking and helps to bring all of the other skills together. If you are fighting for balance during a swing, it's harder to control your club face, path and low point. This can lead to shots that do not match your intention.

Equipment: Mid-iron, balls, notebook, pen

Part 1

- Choose a club and hit 5 balls in each of the following positions:
  - Feet together
  - Balancing on only your left leg
  - Balancing on only your right leg
  - Feet together

Balance	1	2	3	4	5
Feet Together					
Left Leg					
Right Leg					
Feet Together					

Part 2

- Choose a target to aim at.

- Select a club and hit a shot while trying to achieve perfect balance.

- Focus on your balance, not where the ball finishes.

- Hold your finish for 5 seconds.

- Score your balance on every shot on a scale of 1 to 10 (10 = perfect).

- Change clubs after every shot.

- How many shots does it take to achieve 5 10s?

- Record your score. Next time, aim to achieve 5 10s in fewer attempts.

- Every time you set a new personal best, write it down. Be proud of your progress and celebrate your success!

Perfect Balance	1	2	3	4	5	Total
Attempts						

Dr Nicky Lumb & Dr Dave Alred MBE

3 Perfect Strikes

Ball striking is the single biggest differentiator between playing standards. A perfect strike feels amazing! End every technical practice with 3 perfect strikes.

Equipment: Mid-iron, balls, notebook, pen

- Choose a target.

- Select a club.

- Score your strike out of 10 (10 = perfect).

- Change clubs after every shot.

- How many shots does it take to achieve 3 10s?

- Record your score and next time aim to achieve 3 10s in fewer attempts.

- Every time you set a new personal best, write it down. Be proud of your progress and celebrate your success!

Perfect Strikes	1	2	3	Total
Attempts				

APPROACH SHOTS TO THE GREEN - PITCHING

Pitching is all shots between 50 and 100 yards from the green. An approach shot finishing within 10ft of the hole creates a realistic one-putt opportunity, while a shot finishing inside 20ft is generally within two-putt range, so these target sizes are used. If your average proximity to the target is inside 20ft, you may prefer to use that distance. For your practice to be most effective, it should be more demanding than playing on the course, so whatever target size you use, make sure it challenges you.

This section covers practices you can do on a practice ground with your own balls and targets and on a driving range where the balls and targets are provided. It's vital to always measure your shot accuracy, so when you are unable to mark out target zones, use other targets on the range, objects in the background or your best judgement.

If you like to shape the ball from left to right or right to left, you can incorporate it into any practice.

With every practice, you will get the most benefit if you are alert and fully engaged. To make this more likely, any practice can be completed simultaneously with another, so you may want to incorporate a pitching practice with a putting or driving practice so that you change shot types between shots or sets, and move from a training practice towards a more challenging tournament practice.

Dr Nicky Lumb & Dr Dave Alred MBE

Training Practices

Once your technical practice is complete, it's time to focus on golf shots instead of golf swings!

Wedge Matrix Distances

This practice will improve accuracy with your wedges and different swing lengths (¼, ½, ¾, full). The goal is to hit 3 shots inside the target zone (10ft or 20ft) with each wedge and swing length. Based on your skill level, choose the most appropriate target size. You can use a custom target zone if your average proximity to the target is inside 20ft.

Equipment: Wedges, balls, 8 markers, notebook, pen

Level 1

- Choose a flag or create a target.
- Place markers 10ft or 20ft from the target at 12, 3, 6, and 9 o'clock.
- Choose a wedge and place markers at your average hitting distance for each swing length.
- Using a half or 9 o'clock swing, how many shots does it take to hit 3 balls inside the target zone?
- Using a full or 12 o'clock swing, how many shots does it take to hit 3 balls inside the target zone?
- Using a quarter or 7.30 swing, how many shots does it take to hit 3 balls inside the target zone?
- Using a ¾ or 10.30 swing, how many shots does it take to hit 3 balls inside the target zone?
- Repeat using a different wedge.
- Record your scores and next time aim to complete this practice in one shot less. Every time you set a new personal best, write it down. Be proud of your progress and celebrate your success!
- Next time you do this practice, use different wedges.

Dr Nicky Lumb & Dr Dave Alred MBE

Wedge:		Shot No.	1	2	3	Total
Swing Length: Half / 9 o'clock	Distance: Target Size:	Attempts				
Swing Length: Full / 12 o'clock	Distance: Target Size:	Attempts				
Swing Length: ¼ / 7.30	Distance: Target Size:	Attempts				
Swing Length: ¾ / 10.30	Distance: Target Size:	Attempts				
Wedge:		**Shot No.**	**1**	**2**	**3**	**Total**
Swing Length: Half / 9 o'clock	Distance: Target Size:	Attempts				
Swing Length: Full / 12 o'clock	Distance: Target Size:	Attempts				
Swing Length: ¼ / 7.30	Distance: Target Size:	Attempts				
Swing Length: ¾ / 10.30	Distance: Target Size:	Attempts				

Level 2

- Choose a flag or create a target.

- Place markers 10ft from the target at 12, 3, 6, and 9 o'clock.

- Choose a wedge and place markers at your average hitting distance for each swing length.

- Using a half or 9 o'clock swing, how many shots does it take to hit 1 ball inside 10ft?

- Using a full or 12 o'clock swing, how many shots does it take to hit 1 ball inside 10ft?

- Using a quarter or 7.30 swing, how many shots does it take to hit 1 ball inside 10ft?

- Using a ¾ or 10.30 swing, how many shots does it take to hit 1 ball inside 10ft?

- Follow this sequence until you have hit 3 balls inside 10ft with each swing length.

- Repeat using a different wedge.

- Record your scores and next time aim to complete this practice in one shot less. Every time you set a new personal best, write it down. Be proud of your progress and celebrate your success!

- Next time you do this practice, use different wedges.

Wedge:		Shot No.	1	2	3	Total
Swing Length: Half / 9 o'clock	Distance: Target Size:	Attempts				
Swing Length: Full / 12 o'clock	Distance: Target Size:	Attempts				
Swing Length: ¼ / 7.30	Distance: Target Size:	Attempts				
Swing Length: ¾ / 10.30	Distance: Target Size:	Attempts				

Wedge:		Shot No.	1	2	3	Total
Swing Length: Half / 9 o'clock	Distance: Target Size:	Attempts				
Swing Length: Full / 12 o'clock	Distance: Target Size:	Attempts				
Swing Length: ¼ / 7.30	Distance: Target Size:	Attempts				
Swing Length: ¾ / 10.30	Distance: Target Size:	Attempts				

Stock vs. Random Moving – 50-100 yards

On the course, most shots will not match the exact distance you hit one of your wedges, and you will have to adjust your swing. Stock vs. Random practices will help to develop your distance and directional control and better prepare you for these situations. This practice uses your own balls and targets. It focuses on hitting shots from different positions, making it one of the most effective practices in simulating playing golf.

This practice includes two distance bands: 50-75yds and 75-100yds. The stock shots are from more familiar distances: 50, 60, 70, 80, 90 and 100 yards. The random shots can be from any distance between 50 and 100 yards. This design can be adapted and applied to any yardage bands.

Equipment: Wedges, 18 balls, 14 markers, laser rangefinder, notebook, pen

Dr Nicky Lumb & Dr Dave Alred MBE

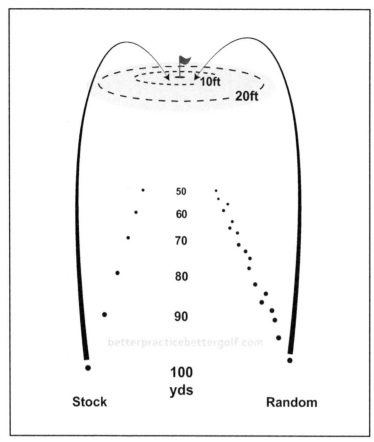

Figure 16. Stock vs. Random Moving Practice

Stock

- Choose a flag or create a target.

- Place markers 10ft and 20ft from the target at 12, 3, 6, and 9 o'clock.

- Put markers at 50, 60, 70, 80, 90 and 100 yards.

- Hit 3 shots from each distance.

- Score 2 points for every shot that finishes inside 10ft and 1 point for every shot that finishes inside 20ft.

- How many points can you score? Record your stock shot total.

- Pick up your balls before hitting the random shots.

Random

- Place 18 balls between the 50- and 100-yard markers so there is one ball every two to three yards.

- In a random order, hit each ball. Aim to have at least a 5-yard gap between each shot.

- Measure the distance of every shot and go through your pre-shot routine.

- Score 2 points for every shot that finishes inside 10ft and 1 point for every shot that finishes inside 20ft.

- Can your random score beat your stock score?

- To introduce pressure, set a target score. If you do not reach it, give yourself one opportunity to hit a shot from 75 yards inside 10ft or 20ft, with a consequence of repeating the practice or choosing an unwelcome penalty.

- Record your scores and next time aim to score more points. Every time you set a new personal best, write it down. Be proud of your progress and celebrate your success!

50-100 yds	Stock		Random	
	10ft	20ft	10ft	20ft
Shots Inside				
Points				
Inside 10ft - Score 2 pts. Inside 20ft - Score 1 pt				

Dr Nicky Lumb & Dr Dave Alred MBE

Short vs. Long Moving – 50-75 yards

On the course, there will be times when your approach shot into the green must stay short or be past the hole. You will be best prepared if you have practiced these situations before. This practice uses your own balls and targets and focuses on hitting shots from different positions making it one of the most effective practices in simulating playing golf.

Equipment: Wedges, 18 balls, 12 markers, laser rangefinder, notebook, pen

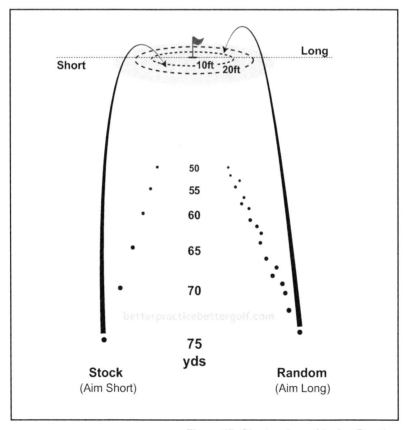

Figure 17. Short vs Long Moving Practice

Stock – Every ball must be short of the target

- Choose a flag or create a target.

- Place markers 10ft and 20ft from the target at 3, 6 and 9 o'clock.

- Put markers at 50, 55, 60, 65, 70 and 75 yards.

- Hit 3 shots from each distance.

- Every ball must stay short of the target to score.

- Score 2 points for every shot that finishes inside 10ft and 1 point for every shot that finishes inside 20ft.

- How many points can you score? Record your stock shot total.

- Pick up your balls before hitting the random shots.

Random – Every ball must be past the target

- Place markers 10ft and 20ft from the target at 3, 9 and 12 o'clock.

- Place 18 balls between the 50- and 75-yard markers so there is one ball every one to two yards.

- In a random order, hit each ball. Aim to have at least a 3-yard gap between each shot.

- Measure the distance of every shot and go through your pre-shot routine.

- Every ball must be past the target to score.

- Score 2 points for every shot that finishes inside 10ft and 1 point for every shot that finishes inside 20ft.

- Can your random score beat your stock score?

- Record your scores and next time aim to score more points. Every time you set a new personal best, write

Dr Nicky Lumb & Dr Dave Alred MBE

it down. Be proud of your progress and celebrate your success!

50-75 yds	Stock Short Only		Random Long Only	
	10ft	20ft	10ft	20ft
Shots Inside				
Points				
Inside 10ft - Score 2 pts. Inside 20ft - Score 1 pt				

Left vs. Right Moving – 75-100 yards

On the course, there will be times when your approach shot into the green must stay left or right of the hole. You will be best prepared if you have practiced these situations before. This practice uses your own balls and targets and focuses on hitting shots from different positions making it one of the most effective practices in simulating playing golf.

If you like to shape the ball from left to right and right to left, hit every ball that must finish right with a fade and every shot that must finish left with a draw.

Equipment: Wedges, 18 balls, 12 markers, laser rangefinder, notebook, pen

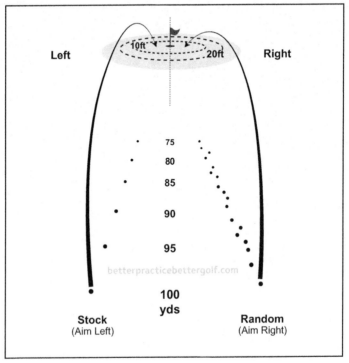

Figure 18. Left vs. Right Moving Practice

Dr Nicky Lumb & Dr Dave Alred MBE

Stock – Every ball must be left of the target

- Choose a flag or create a target.
- Place markers 10ft and 20ft from the target at 12, 3 and 6 o'clock.
- Every ball must be left of the target to score.
- Put markers at 75, 80, 85, 90, 95 and 100 yards.
- Hit 3 shots from each distance.
- Score 2 points for every shot that finishes inside 10ft and 1 point for every shot that finishes inside 20ft.
- How many points can you score? Record your stock shot total.
- Pick up your balls before hitting the random shots.

Random – Every ball must be right of the target

- Place markers 10ft and 20ft from the target at 12, 6 and 9 o'clock.
- Every ball must be right of the target to score.
- Place 18 balls between the 75- and 100-yard markers so there is one ball every one to two yards.
- In a random order, hit each ball. Aim to have at least a 3-yard gap between each shot.
- Measure the distance of every shot and go through your pre-shot routine.
- Score 2 points for every shot that finishes inside 10ft and 1 point for every shot that finishes inside 20ft.
- Can your random score beat your stock score?
- Record your scores and next time aim to score more points. Every time you set a new personal best, write

it down. Be proud of your progress and celebrate your success!

75-100 yds Left vs. Right	Stock Left Only		Random Right Only	
	10ft	20ft	10ft	20ft
Shots Inside				
Points				
Inside 10ft - Score 2 pts. Inside 20ft - Score 1 pt				

Stock vs. Random Static – 50-100 yards

On the course, most shots will not match the exact distance you hit one of your wedges and you will have to adjust your swing. Stock vs. Random practices will help to develop your distance and directional control and better prepare you for these situations. This practice uses your own balls and targets and focuses on hitting from a practice tee.

This practice includes two distance bands: 50-75yds and 75-100yds. The stock shots are from more familiar distances: 50, 60, 70, 80, 90 and 100 yards. The random shots can be from any distance between 50 and 100 yards.

Equipment: Wedges, balls, 8 markers, laser rangefinder, notebook, pen

(Use a launch monitor to receive carry distance and accuracy feedback after every shot if you have access to one).

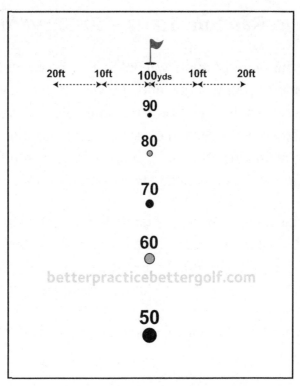

Figure 19. Stock vs. Random Static Practice

Level 1

Stock

- Place markers at 50, 60, 70, 80, 90 and 100 yards in a relatively straight line. It's easiest if you have at least 2 different coloured markers so you can alternate between colours every 10 yards.

- Choose a target size (e.g. 10ft or 20ft). The target size should be challenging but achievable. At 100 yards, place markers on either side of the target at that distance so you can judge if each ball lands directionally inside them. There are 10 yards (30ft) between each distance marker to help you judge the distance and if each ball lands inside the target zone.

Dr Nicky Lumb & Dr Dave Alred MBE

- Hit 3 shots to each target. Continue this process until 9 shots have landed within the target zone. Use a tally chart to mark every shot on the scorecard.

- How many shots does it take for 9 balls to land in the target zone? Record your stock shot total.

Random

- Use a random number app to generate different numbers between 50 and 100. These will be your shot distances.

- Using the targets in place from the stock shots, use your best judgement to determine your accuracy.

- Go through your pre-shot routine before every shot.

- How many shots does it take for 9 balls to land in the target zone?

- Can your random score beat your stock score?

- Put yourself under pressure by setting a target for the number of attempts you have to complete the practice. If it takes more, give yourself one opportunity to hit a shot within 10ft or 20ft of 100 yards, with a consequence of repeating the practice or choosing an unwelcome penalty.

- Record your scores and next time aim to complete the practice in less shots. Every time you set a new personal best, write it down. Be proud of your progress and celebrate your success!

50-100 yds Target Size:	Stock	Random
Shots Inside Target Zone	9	9
Attempts		

Level 2

- Immediately after hitting each ball predict if the ball will land inside the scoring zone.

- Score how many predictions you get right.

50-100 yds Target Size:	Stock	Random
Shots Inside Target Zone	9	9
Attempts		
Successful Predictions		

Left vs. Right Static – 75-100 yards

On the course, there will be times when your approach shots into the green must stay left or right of the hole. You will be best prepared if you have practiced these situations before.

If you like to shape the ball from left to right and right to left, hit every ball that must finish right with a fade and every shot that must finish left with a draw.

Equipment: Wedges, balls, 8 markers, laser rangefinder, notebook, pen

(Use a launch monitor to receive carry distance and accuracy feedback after every shot if you have access to one).

Stock – Every ball must land and finish left of the target

- Place markers at 75, 80, 85, 90, 95 and 100 yards in a relatively straight line. It's easiest if you have at least 2 different coloured markers so you can alternate between colours every 10 yards.

- Choose a target size (e.g. 10ft or 20ft). The target size should be challenging but achievable. At 100 yards, place markers on either side of the target at that distance so you can judge if each ball lands directionally inside them. There are 5 yards (15ft) between each distance marker to help you judge the distance and if each ball lands inside the target zone.

- Hit 3 shots to each target.

- Continue this process until 9 shots have landed within the target zone.

- Every ball must be left of the target to score.

- Use a tally chart to mark every shot on the scorecard.

- How many shots does it take for 9 balls to land in the target zone? Record your stock shot total.

Random – Every ball must land and finish right of the hole

- Use a random number app to generate different numbers between 75 and 100. These are your shot distances.

- Using the targets in place from the stock shots, use your best judgement to determine your accuracy.

- Go through your pre-shot routine before every shot.

- How many shots does it take for 9 balls to land in the target zone?

- Every ball must be right of the target to score.

- Can your random score beat your stock score?

- Put yourself under pressure by setting a target for the number of attempts you have to complete the practice. If it takes more, give yourself one opportunity to hit a shot within 10ft or 20ft of 75 yards, with a consequence of repeating the practice or choosing an unwelcome penalty.

- Record your scores and next time aim to complete the practice in less shots. Every time you set a new personal best, write it down. Be proud of your progress and celebrate your success!

75-100 yds Target Size:	Stock Left Only	Random Right Only
Shots Inside Target Zone	9	9
Attempts		

Dr Nicky Lumb & Dr Dave Alred MBE

APPROACH SHOTS TO THE GREEN - IRONS

Approach shots into the green are the most important shots in golf. Iron shot accuracy accounts for 40% of the difference between varying playing standards. Hitting more greens generally means lower scores. Hitting just one green more than your average usually saves 1.5 shots a round, so let's get your iron game as accurate as possible!

With every practice, choose a challenging but appropriate target size. An approach shot finishing within 10ft of the hole creates a realistic one-putt opportunity, while a shot finishing inside 30ft is generally within two-putt range, so these target sizes are used. If your average proximity to the target is inside 30ft, you may prefer to use that distance. For your practice to be most effective, it should be more demanding than playing on the course, so whatever target size you decide to use, make sure it challenges you, and over time aim to reduce it.

It's usually easier to improve accuracy with shorter irons than longer ones, so all of the iron practices start at one hundred yards and incorporate one (100-125 yards) or two yardage bands (100-125 yards and 125-150 yards). Everyone hits the ball different distances, so if these distances don't incorporate a pitching wedge, 9 iron or 8 iron, change the distances so that they do. Once you feel competent from these distances and using these clubs, copy the template from any practice and adjust it so that you spend most of your time working on the yardage bands you play from the most on the course.

This section covers practices you can do on a practice ground with your own balls and targets and on a driving range where the balls and targets are provided. It's vital to always measure your shot accuracy, so when you are unable to mark out target zones, use other targets on the range, objects in the background or your best judgement.

If you like to shape the ball from left to right or right to left, you can incorporate it into any practice.

With every practice, you will get the most benefit if you are alert and fully engaged. To make this more likely, any practice can be completed simultaneously with another, so you may want to incorporate an iron practice with a putting or chipping practice so that you change shot types between shots or sets and move from a training practice towards a more challenging tournament practice.

Training Practices

Iron Matrix Distances

This practice will improve your accuracy with your iron shot matrix distances.

Equipment: Irons, balls, markers, notebook, pen

(Use a launch monitor to receive carry distance and accuracy feedback after every shot if you have access to one).

Level 1

- Place markers at your average hitting distance for a 9, 8 and 7 iron. If you cannot use your own markers, use targets on the range that most closely fit your yardages and use your best judgement to determine your accuracy.

- Choose a target size for each iron, e.g. 10ft or 30ft (or your average proximity to the target if it is inside 30ft). The target size should be challenging but achievable.

- How many shots does it take to land:
    - 3 balls inside 10ft or 30ft with your 9 iron?
    - 3 balls inside 10ft or 30ft with your 8 iron?
    - 3 balls inside 10ft or 30ft with your 7 iron?

- Mark the scorecard every time a ball lands inside the scoring zone.

- Record your scores and next time aim to score one shot better with each iron. Every time you set a new personal best, write it down. Be proud of your progress and celebrate your success!

- To stay mentally fresh, when you have hit 3 shots to one target, do a set of a putting or short game practice before returning to the driving range.

		Shot No.	1	2	3	Total
Iron: 9	Distance: Target Size:	Attempts				
Iron: 8	Distance: Target Size:	Attempts				
Iron: 7	Distance: Target Size:	Attempts				

Level 2

- Place markers at your average hitting distance for a 9, 8 and 7 iron. If you cannot use your own markers, use targets on the range that most closely fit your yardages.

- How many shots does it take to land:

   ◦ 1 ball inside 10ft or 30ft with your 9 iron?

   ◦ 1 ball inside 10ft or 30ft with your 8 iron?

   ◦ 1 ball inside 10ft or 30ft with your 7 iron?

- Continue this process until you have hit 3 balls with each club inside 10ft or 30ft.

- Mark the scorecard every time a ball lands inside the scoring zone.

- Record your scores and next time aim to score one shot better with each iron. Every time you set a new personal best, write it down. Be proud of your progress and celebrate your success!

		Shot No.	1	2	3	Total
Iron: 9	Distance: Target Size:	Attempts				
Iron: 8	Distance: Target Size:	Attempts				
Iron: 7	Distance: Target Size:	Attempts				

Level 3

- Place markers at your average hitting distance for a pitching wedge, 9, 8, 7, 6 and 5 iron. If you cannot use your own markers, use targets on the range that most closely fit your yardages.

- How many shots does it take to land:

  - 3 balls inside 10ft or 20ft with your pitching wedge?
  - 3 balls inside 10ft or 30ft with your 6 iron?
  - 3 balls inside 10ft or 30ft with your 8 iron?
  - 3 balls inside 10ft or 30ft with your 5 iron?
  - 3 balls inside 10ft or 30ft with your 9 iron?
  - 3 balls inside 10ft or 30ft with your 7 iron?

- Mark the scorecard every time a ball lands inside the scoring zone.

- Record your scores and next time aim to score one shot better with each iron. Every time you set a new personal best, write it down. Be proud of your progress and celebrate your success!

		Shot No.	1	2	3	Total
Wedge: PW	Distance: Target Size:	Attempts				
Iron: 9	Distance: Target Size:	Attempts				
Iron: 8	Distance: Target Size:	Attempts				
Iron: 7	Distance: Target Size:	Attempts				
Iron: 6	Distance: Target Size:	Attempts				
Iron: 5	Distance: Target Size:	Attempts				

Dr Nicky Lumb & Dr Dave Alred MBE

Stock vs. Random Moving – 100-150 yards

On the course, most shots will not match the exact distance you hit a club, so you will have to adjust your swing. Stock vs. Random practices will help you to develop your distance and directional control and better prepare you for these situations. This practice uses your own balls and targets and focuses on hitting shots from different positions making it very effective in simulating playing golf.

This practice includes two distance bands: 100-125yds and 125-150yds. The stock shots are from more familiar distances: 100, 110, 120, 130, 140 and 150 yards. The random shots can be from any distance between 100 and 150 yards. This practice design can be adapted and applied to any yardage bands.

Equipment: Wedges / irons, 18 balls, 14 markers, laser rangefinder, notebook, pen

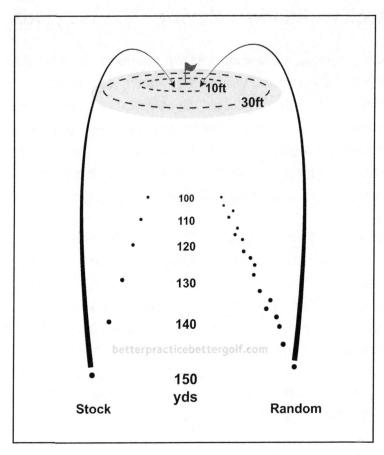

Figure 20. Stock vs. Random Moving Practice

Stock

- Choose a flag or create a target.

- Place markers 10ft and 30ft from the target at 12, 3, 6 and 9 o'clock.

- Put markers at 100, 110, 120, 130, 140 and 150 yards.

- Hit 3 shots from each distance.

- Score 2 points for every shot that finishes inside 10ft and 1 point for every shot that finishes inside 30ft.

Dr Nicky Lumb & Dr Dave Alred MBE

- How many points can you score? Record your stock shot total.

- Pick up your balls before hitting the random shots.

Random

- Place 18 balls between the 100- and 150-yard markers so there is one ball every two to three yards.

- In a random order, hit each ball. Aim to have at least a 5-yard gap between each shot.

- Measure the distance of every shot and go through your pre-shot routine.

- Score 2 points for every shot that finishes inside 10ft and 1 point for every shot that finishes inside 30ft.

- Can your random score beat your stock score?

- To introduce pressure, set a target score. If you do not reach it, give yourself one opportunity to hit a shot from 120 yards inside 10ft or 30ft, with a consequence of repeating the practice or choosing an unwelcome penalty.

- Record your scores and next time aim to score more points. Every time you set a new personal best, write it down. Be proud of your progress and celebrate your success!

100-150 yds	Stock		Random	
	10ft	30ft	10ft	30ft
Shots Inside				
Points				
Inside 10ft - Score 2 pts. Inside 30ft - Score 1 pt				

Stock vs. Random Static – 100-150 yards

This practice uses your own balls and targets and focuses on hitting from a practice tee. The template can be adapted and applied to any yardage bands.

Equipment: Wedges / irons, balls, 8 markers, laser rangefinder, notebook, pen

(Use a launch monitor to receive carry distance and accuracy feedback after every shot if you have access to one).

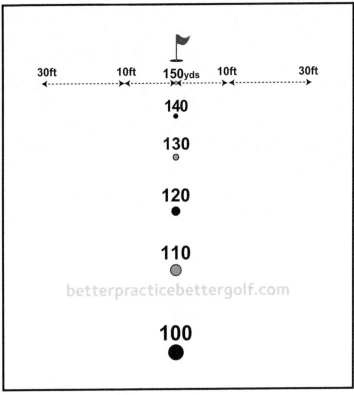

Figure 21. Stock vs. Random Static Practice

Dr Nicky Lumb & Dr Dave Alred MBE

Level 1

Stock

- Place markers at 100, 110, 120, 130, 140 and 150 yards in a relatively straight line. It's easiest if you have at least 2 different coloured markers so you can alternate between colours every 10 yards.

- Choose a target size (e.g. 10ft or 30ft). The target size should be challenging but achievable. At 150 yards, place markers on either side of the target at that distance so you can judge if each ball lands directionally inside them. There are 10 yards (30ft) between each distance marker to help you judge the distance and if each ball lands inside 10ft or 30ft.

- Hit 3 shots to each target. Continue this process until 9 shots have landed within the target zone. Use a tally chart to mark every shot on the scorecard.

- How many shots does it take for 9 balls to land in the target zone? Record your stock shot total.

Random

- Use a random number app to generate different numbers between 100 and 150. These will be your shot distances.

- Using the targets in place from the stock shots, use your best judgement to determine your accuracy.

- Go through your pre-shot routine before every shot.

- How many shots does it take for 9 balls to land in the target zone?

- Can your random score beat your stock score?

- Put yourself under pressure by setting a target for the number of attempts you have to complete the practice.

If it takes more, give yourself one opportunity to hit a shot within your target distance of 150 yards, with a consequence of repeating the practice or choosing an unwelcome penalty.

- Record your scores and next time aim to score more points. Every time you set a new personal best, write it down. Be proud of your progress and celebrate your success!

Level 2

- Immediately after hitting each ball predict if the ball will land inside the scoring zone.

- Score how many predictions you get right.

100-150 yds Target Size:	Stock	Random
Shots Inside Target Zone	9	9
Attempts		
Successful Predictions		

Dr Nicky Lumb & Dr Dave Alred MBE

Stock vs. Random Static – 150-200 yards

This practice uses your own balls and targets and focuses on hitting from a practice tee. The template can be adapted and applied to any yardage bands.

Equipment: Wedges / irons, balls, 8 markers, laser rangefinder, notebook, pen

(Use a launch monitor to receive carry distance and accuracy feedback after every shot if you have access to one).

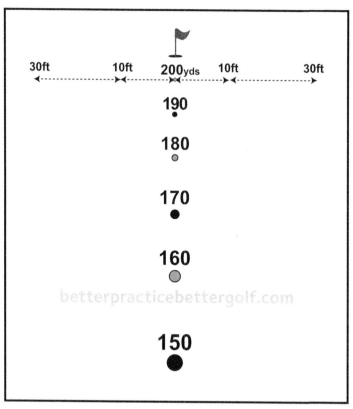

Figure 22. Stock vs. Random Static Practice

Level 1

Stock

- Place markers at 150, 160, 170, 180, 190 and 200 yards in a relatively straight line. It's easiest if you have at least 2 different coloured markers so you can alternate between colours every 10 yards.

- Choose a target size (e.g. 10ft or 30ft). The target size should be challenging but achievable. At 200 yards, place markers on either side of the target at that distance so you can judge if each ball lands directionally inside them. There are 10 yards (30ft) between each distance marker to help you judge the distance and if each ball lands inside 10ft or 30ft.

- Hit 3 shots to each target. Continue this process until 9 shots have landed within the target zone. Use a tally chart to mark every shot on the scorecard.

- How many shots does it take for 9 balls to land in the target zone? Record your stock shot total.

Random

- Use a random number app to generate different numbers between 150 and 200. These will be your shot distances.

- Using the targets in place from the stock shots, use your best judgement to determine your accuracy.

- Go through your pre-shot routine before every shot.

- How many shots does it take for 9 balls to land in the target zone?

- Can your random score beat your stock score?

- Put yourself under pressure by setting a target for the number of attempts you have to complete the practice. If

Dr Nicky Lumb & Dr Dave Alred MBE

it takes more, give yourself one opportunity to hit a shot within 10ft or 30ft of 170 yards, with a consequence of repeating the practice or choosing an unwelcome penalty.

- Record your scores and next time aim to score more points. Every time you set a new personal best, write it down. Be proud of your progress and celebrate your success!

Level 2

- Immediately after hitting each ball predict if the ball will land inside the scoring zone.

- Score how many predictions you get right.

150-200 yds Target Size:	Stock	Random
Shots Inside Target Zone	9	9
Attempts		
Successful Predictions		

Stock vs. Random Launch Monitor – 100-150 yards

A launch monitor gives immediate feedback, and knowing the carry distance of every shot as soon as each ball lands can accelerate your learning and distance control. To get the most benefit, after hitting each ball, immediately predict its landing distance, then check the distance on the launch monitor software. Some launch monitors such as Trackman have a voice system that will tell you the carry distance after each shot. This practice can be adapted and applied to any yardage bands.

Equipment: Wedges / irons, balls, 8 markers, laser rangefinder, launch monitor, notebook, pen

Level 1

Stock

- Place markers at 100, 110, 120, 130, 140 and 150 yards or use markers on the driving range that are closest to these distances.

- Choose a target size, e.g. 10ft or 30ft (or your average proximity to the target if it is inside 30ft). The target size should be challenging but achievable.

- Hit 3 balls to each target. Continue this process until 9 shots have landed within the target zone.

- Use a tally chart to mark every successful shot on the scorecard.

- How many shots does it take for 9 balls to land in the target zone? Record your stock shot total.

Dr Nicky Lumb & Dr Dave Alred MBE

Random

- Set the launch monitor to create random distances between 100 and 150 yards. If the system does not do this, use a random number generator app.

- Go through your pre-shot routine before every shot.

- How many shots does it take for 9 balls to land in the target zone?

- Can your random score beat your stock score?

- Put yourself under pressure by setting a target for the number of attempts you have to complete the practice. If it takes more, give yourself one opportunity to hit a shot within 10ft or 30ft of 150 yards, with a consequence of repeating the practice or choosing an unwelcome penalty.

- Record your scores and next time aim to complete this practice in less shots. Every time you set a new personal best, write it down. Be proud of your progress and celebrate your success!

100-150 yds Target Size:	Stock	Random
Successful Shots	9	9
Attempts		

Level 2

- Immediately after hitting each ball predict its landing distance. Then check your prediction on the launch monitor software.

- How many of your predictions were within 5 yards?

- Over time as your distance predictions improve, score them within 3 yards.

100-150 yds Target Size:	Stock	Random
Successful Shots	9	9
Attempts		
Successful Predictions		

9-Ball Distance Challenge

The 9-ball distance challenge will develop your distance and directional control. It is relatively easy to do at any practice facility that provides balls and targets, you will just need to use your best judgement to determine your accuracy if you do not have access to a launch monitor or distance feedback device.

This template can be used at any distance, and you can adjust the size of the scoring zone to best suit your needs.

Equipment: Irons / wedges, balls, laser rangefinder, notebook, pen

(Use a launch monitor to receive carry distance and accuracy feedback after every shot if you have access to one).

Level 1

- Choose a target at 125 yards.

- Choose a target size, e.g. 10ft or 30ft (or your average proximity to the target if it is inside 30ft). The target size should be challenging but achievable.

- How many shots does it take to land:

    ○ 3 balls inside 10ft or 30ft at 125 yards?

    ○ 3 balls inside 10ft or 30ft and 5 yards short at 120 yards?

    ○ 3 balls inside 10ft or 30ft and 5 yards long at 130 yards?

- Mark the scorecard every time a ball lands inside the scoring zone.

- Record your scores and next time aim to be one shot better. Every time you set a new personal best, write it down. Be proud of your progress and celebrate your success!

- If you start at 30ft, when you can complete this practice in 18 shots or less, reduce the scoring zone by 5ft. Over time, how small can you make it?

Target Size:	Target 125yds	Short 120yds	Long 130yds	Total
Shots in Target Zone	3	3	3	9
Attempts				

Level 2

- Choose a target at 125 yards.

- How many shots does it take to land:
  - 3 balls inside 10ft or 30ft at 125 yards?
  - 2 balls inside 10ft or 30ft and 5 yards short at 120 yards?
  - 2 balls inside 10ft or 30ft at 125 yards?
  - 2 balls inside 10ft or 30ft and 5 yards long at 130 yards?

- Mark the scorecard every time a ball lands inside the scoring zone.

- Record your scores and next time aim to be one shot better. Every time you set a new personal best, write it down. Be proud of your progress and celebrate your success!

Dr Nicky Lumb & Dr Dave Alred MBE

- If you start at 30ft, when you can complete this practice in 18 shots or less, reduce the scoring zone by 5ft. Over time, how small can you make it?

Target Size:	Target 125yds	Short 120yds	Target 125yds	Long 130yds	Total
Shots in Target Zone	3	2	2	2	9
Attempts					

Level 3

- Choose a target at 125 yards.
- How many shots does it take to land:
  - 1 ball inside 10ft or 30ft at 125 yards?
  - 1 ball inside 10ft or 30ft and 5 yards short at 120 yards?
  - 1 ball inside 10ft or 30ft and 5 yards long at 130 yards?
  - 1 ball inside 10ft or 30ft at 125 yards?
  - 1 ball inside 10ft or 30ft and 5 yards short at 120 yards?
  - 1 ball inside 10ft or 30ft and 5 yards long at 130 yards?
  - 1 ball inside 10ft or 30ft at 125 yards?
  - 1 ball inside 10ft or 30ft and 5 yards short at 120 yards?
  - 1 ball inside 10ft or 30ft and 5 yards long at 130 yards?
- Mark the scorecard every time a ball lands inside the scoring zone.

- Put yourself under pressure by setting a target for the number of attempts you have to complete the practice. If it takes more, give yourself one opportunity to hit one shot within 10ft or 20ft of 100 yards, with a consequence of repeating the practice or choosing an unwelcome penalty.

- Record your scores and next time aim to be one shot better. Every time you set a new personal best, write it down. Be proud of your progress and celebrate your success!

- If you start at 30ft, when you can complete this practice in 18 shots or less, reduce the scoring zone by 5ft. Over time, how small can you make it?

Target Size:	Target 125yd	Short 120yd	Long 130yd	Target 125yd	Short 120yd	Long 130yd	Target 125yd	Short 120yd	Long 130yd	Total
Shots in Target Zone	1	1	1	1	1	1	1	1	1	9
Attempts										

Dr Nicky Lumb & Dr Dave Alred MBE

5 Shots with 5 Different Targets

Equipment: All of your clubs, balls, tees, laser rangefinder, notebook, pen

(Use a launch monitor to receive carry distance and accuracy feedback after every shot if you have access to one).

Level 1

- Choose a target within range for a wedge and measure the distance. Use your best judgment to determine your accuracy.

- How many shots does it take to hit one ball inside 20ft?

- Choose a target within range for a short iron and measure the distance.

- How many shots does it take to hit one ball inside 30ft?

- Choose a target within range for a mid-iron and measure the distance.

- How many shots does it take to hit one ball inside 30ft?

- Choose a target within range for a long iron or hybrid and measure the distance.

- How many shots does it take to hit one ball inside 30ft?

- Choose a target for a driver and a minimum distance the ball must fly or choose a target the ball must fly over.

- How many shots does it take to hit one ball inside 20 yards and over the required distance or target?

- Record your scores and next time aim to be one shot better. Every time you set a new personal best, write it down. Be proud of your progress and celebrate your success!

Club	Accuracy	Target Distance	Attempts
Wedge	20ft		
Short Iron	30ft		
Mid-Iron	30ft		
Long Iron or Hybrid	30ft		
Driver	20yds		
Total			

Level 2

- How many shots does it take to hit one ball inside each target zone in consecutive shots?

- If any shot lands outside the scoring zone, start again.

- Record your scores and next time aim to complete the sequence in fewer attempts. Every time you set a new personal best, write it down. Be proud of your progress and celebrate your success!

Club	Accuracy	Target Distance	Attempts
Wedge	20ft		
Short Iron	30ft		
Mid-Iron	30ft		
Long Iron or Hybrid	30ft		
Driver	20yds		
Total			

- When you can consistently complete this practice in consecutive shots, increase the challenge by reducing the scoring zone by 5ft for the wedge and iron shots and 5 yards for your driver. Over time, how small can you make it?

Dr Nicky Lumb & Dr Dave Alred MBE

OFF THE TEE

Most courses have 14 par fours or par fives, and a golfer usually uses their driver 10 to 14 times during a round. The longer a hole is, the more strokes it takes to hole out. When hole design allows, hitting the ball as far as possible off the tee while keeping it in play and giving yourself a clear shot into the green is vital to lower scores. On every driving practice, choose a minimum distance the ball should fly or set a target for the ball to fly over in order to score so that straight mishits that don't fly very far don't count.

The average fairway is between 35 and 45 yards wide for club golfers. This reduces to between 30 and 32 yards for PGA Tour events and can drop to 25 yards for major championships, so all of the practices are based around these numbers. On the PGA Tour, players are generally 30% more accurate with their shots into the green from the fairway than the rough, and this number increases for amateur golfers. This highlights the need to maximize distance whilst maintaining accuracy.

On the course, some golfers always play with one shot shape. Others move the ball from left to right (fade) and right to left (draw). If this is your preference, you can add a shot shape requirement to any practice.

With every practice, you will get the most benefit if you are alert and fully engaged. To make this more likely, any practice can be completed simultaneously with another, so you may want to incorporate a putting or chipping practice so that you change shot types between shots or sets and more closely replicate what you do on the course.

Training Practices

How Many Drives to Hit 14 Fairways?

Equipment: Driver, balls, tees, putter, notebook, pen

(Use a launch monitor to receive carry distance and accuracy feedback after every shot if you have access to one).

Level 1

- Choose a small, precise target.

- Create or imagine a 40-yards-wide fairway (20 yards on either side of the target) using targets on the range, objects in the background, or your best judgement.

- Set a minimum distance the ball must fly or choose a target the ball must fly over (an accurate very short mishit does not count!).

- Go through your pre-shot routine before every drive.

- Mark on the scorecard every time a drive hits the fairway.

- If a ball finishes too far left or right, note it so you become more aware of your shot tendencies.

- How many drives does it take to hit 14 fairways?

- Keep your supply of balls away from you so you have to fetch your next ball.

- Record your scores and next time aim to hit 14 fairways in fewer attempts. Every time you set a new personal best, write it down. Be proud of your progress and celebrate your success!

Dr Nicky Lumb & Dr Dave Alred MBE

- When you can hit 14 fairways in 20 attempts or less three times, increase the challenge by narrowing the fairway by 5 yards. Over time, how narrow can you make it?

Drivers Fairway Size:	1	2	3	4	5	6	7	8	9	10	11	12	13	14	Total
Fairway Hit															14
Too Far Left															
Too Far Right															
Totals	Fairways Hit: 14				Too Far Left:				Too Far Right:					

Level 2

- Choose a small, precise target.

- Create or imagine a 40-yards-wide fairway (20 yards on either side of the target).

- Set a minimum distance the ball must fly or choose a target the ball must fly over.

- Go through your pre-shot routine and hit a drive.

- Mark on the scorecard where the ball finishes: fairway hit, too far left or too far right.

- After every drive that hits the fairway, you must hole a 4ft putt on your first attempt for the drive to count.

- Select a new target.

- How many drives and putts does it take to hit 14 fairways and hole 14 4ft putts on your first attempt?

- Record your scores and next time aim to complete the practice in fewer shots. Every time you set a new personal best, write it down. Be proud of your progress and celebrate your success!

- When you can hit 14 fairways in 20 attempts or less three times, increase the challenge by narrowing the fairway by 5 yards. Over time, how narrow can you make it?

Drivers Fairway Size:	1	2	3	4	5	6	7	8	9	10	11	12	13	14	Total
Fairway Hit															14
Too Far Left															
Too Far Right															
4ft Putt Holed (1st Attempt)															
Totals	Fairways Hit: 14				Too Far Left:			Too Far Right:			4ft Putts Holed:			

Hitting Fairways and Greens

On the course you will often hit a driver off the tee and use an iron to hit your approach shots into greens. This practice will improve both of these skills.

Equipment: All of your clubs, balls, tees, notebook, pen

(Use a launch monitor to receive carry distance and accuracy feedback after every shot if you have access to one).

Level 1

- Choose a small, precise target.

- Create or imagine a 40-yards-wide fairway (20 yards on either side of the target) using targets on the range, objects in the background, or your best judgement.

- Set a minimum distance the ball must fly or choose a target the ball must fly over (an accurate very short mishit does not count!).

- Go through your pre-shot routine and hit a drive.

- Mark on the scorecard where the ball finishes: fairway hit, too far left or too far right.

- Continue this process until you have hit the fairway.

- Choose a small, precise target within range for an iron and measure the distance.

- Create or imagine a 60-feet-wide green (30 feet either side of the target).

- Go through your pre-shot routine and hit the iron shot.

- Mark on the scorecard where the ball finishes: green hit, too far left, too far right, too long or too short.

- Continue this process until you have hit the green.

- Select a new target, hit a drive and continue this process.

- Rotate through your irons so you replicate what you do on the course.

- How many shots does it take to hit 5 fairways and 5 greens?

- Put yourself under pressure by setting a target for the number of shots you have to complete the practice. If it takes more, give yourself one opportunity to hit a fairway and green in consecutive shots on your next attempt, with a consequence of repeating the practice or choosing an unwelcome penalty.

- Record your scores and next time aim to hit 5 fairways and 5 greens in less shots. Every time you set a new personal best, write it down. Be proud of your progress and celebrate your success!

Drives						
Fairway Size:	**1**	**2**	**3**	**4**	**5**	**Total**
Fairway Hit						
Too Left						
Too Right						

Fairways Hit: 5	Too Left:	Too Right:

Irons						
Green Size:	**1**	**2**	**3**	**4**	**5**	**Total**
Green Hit						
Too Left						
Too Right						
Too Short						
Too Long						

Greens Hit: 5	Too Left:	Too Right:
	Too Short:	Too Long:

Level 2

- How many shots does it take to hit 10 fairways and 10 greens?

- Record your scores and next time aim to hit 10 fairways and 10 greens in less shots. Every time you set a new personal best, write it down. Be proud of your progress and celebrate your success!

Drives											
Fairway Size:	*1*	*2*	*3*	*4*	*5*	*6*	*7*	*8*	*9*	*10*	*Total*
Fairway Hit											
Too Left											
Too Right											

Fairways Hit: 14	Too Left:	Too Right:

Irons											
Green Size:	*1*	*2*	*3*	*4*	*5*	*6*	*7*	*8*	*9*	*10*	*Total*
Green Hit											
Too Left											
Too Right											
Too Short											
Too Long											

Greens Hit: 14	Too Left:	Too Right:	Too Short:	Too Long:

Level 3

- Create or imagine a 30-yards-wide fairway (15 yards on either side of the target) using targets on the range, objects in the background, or your best judgement.

- How many shots does it take to hit 14 fairways and 14 greens?

- Record your scores and next time aim to hit 14 fairways and 14 greens in less shots. Every time you set a new personal best, write it down. Be proud of your progress and celebrate your success!

Drives															
Fairway Size:	1	2	3	4	5	6	7	8	9	10	11	12	13	14	Total
Fairway Hit															
Too Left															
Too Right															

Fairways Hit: 14	Too Left:	Too Right:

Irons															
Green Size:	1	2	3	4	5	6	7	8	9	10	11	12	13	14	Total
Green Hit															
Too Left															
Too Right															
Too Short															
Too Long															

Greens Hit: 14	Too Left:	Too Right:	Too Short:	Too Long:

Fairway Woods and Hybrids

At times, fairways can be narrow or there may be a sharp dog leg, which makes hitting a fairway wood or hybrid a better option. This practice will prepare you for these situations.

Equipment: Fairway woods, balls, hybrids, tees, notebook, pen

(Use a launch monitor to receive carry distance and accuracy feedback after every shot if you have access to one).

Level 1

- Choose a small, precise target.

- Create or imagine a 30-yards-wide fairway (15 yards on either side of the target).

- Use your best judgement to determine your accuracy.

- How many shots does it take to hit:

  ○ One fairway wood off a tee into the fairway?

  ○ One hybrid off a tee into the fairway?

- Continue this process until you have hit 5 shots with each club into the fairway.

- Mark the scorecard after each shot.

- Record your scores and next time aim to complete this practice in one shot less. Every time you set a new personal best, write it down. Be proud of your progress and celebrate your success!

Dr Nicky Lumb & Dr Dave Alred MBE

- When you can complete this practice in 15 shots or less, reduce the fairway width by 5 yards. Over time, how narrow can you make it?

Fairway Width:	Shot					
Fairway Woods (Off the Tee)	1	2	3	4	5	Total
Attempts						
Hybrids (Off the Tee)						
Attempts						

Level 2

- To improve the accuracy of your longer approach shots into greens, repeat this practice while hitting your fairway woods and hybrids off the ground.

- Create or imagine a 60-feet-wide green (30 feet on either side of the target).

- Mark the scorecard after each shot.

- Record your scores and next time aim to complete this practice in one shot less. Every time you set a new personal best, write it down. Be proud of your progress and celebrate your success!

Fairway Width:	Shot					
Fairway Woods (Off the Ground)	1	2	3	4	5	Total
Attempts						
Hybrids (Off the Ground)						
Attempts						

18 Tee Shots

Equipment: All of your clubs, 18 balls, tees, notebook, pen

(Use a launch monitor to receive carry distance and accuracy feedback after every shot if you have access to one).

- Choose a small, precise target.

- Use targets on the range, objects in the background or your best judgement to determine your accuracy.

- Set a minimum distance the ball must fly or choose a target the ball must fly over (an accurate very short mishit does not count!).

- Follow the shot order on the scorecard. The practice consists of 18 tee shots: 12 drives (D), 2 fairway woods (FW), 2 hybrids (HY) and 2 irons (I).

- Go through your pre-shot routine before every tee shot.

- Use the scoring system to score your accuracy. Fill in the scorecard after every shot.

- To introduce pressure, set a target score. If you do not reach it, give yourself one opportunity to hit a drive within 20 yards of a target followed by an iron off the ground to within 30ft of a target, with a consequence of repeating the practice or choosing an unwelcome penalty.

- Record your total score and next time aim to score more points. Every time you set a new personal best, write it down. Be proud of your progress and celebrate your success!

Dr Nicky Lumb & Dr Dave Alred MBE

Scoring System

Club	Inside 10ft	Inside 20ft	Inside 30ft/10yds	Inside 15yds	Inside 20yds
Driver	5	4	3	2	1
Fwy / Hybrid	4	3	2	1	0
Iron	3	2	1	0	0

Shot	1	2	3	4	5	6	7	8	9	Total
Club	D	D	I	D	D	FW	D	HY	D	
Score										

Shot	10	11	12	13	14	15	16	17	18	Total
Club	D	I	D	FW	D	D	HY	D	D	
Score										
							Final Total:			

THROUGH THE BAG

Tournament Practices

Every shot in this section is unique, just as each shot is on the course.

Fairways and Greens

On the course after every tee shot, you will use a different club next. This practice will improve your long game skills.

Equipment: All of your clubs, 28 balls, tees, notebook, pen

(Use a launch monitor to receive carry distance and accuracy feedback after every shot if you have access to one).

- Choose a small, precise target.
- Use targets on the range, objects in the background or your best judgement to determine your accuracy.
- Set a minimum distance the ball must fly or choose a target the ball must fly over (an accurate very short mishit does not count!).
- Go through your pre-shot routine and hit a drive.
- Use the scoring system to score your accuracy. Fill in the scorecard after every shot.
- Choose a small, precise target within range for a short-iron and measure the distance.
- Go through your pre-shot routine, hit the iron shot and score your accuracy.
- Select a new target and hit a drive.

Dr Nicky Lumb & Dr Dave Alred MBE

- Repeat this sequence for 14 drives and 14 iron shots.

- Rotate through all of the irons in your bag.

- Note if there is a tendency to miss shots left or right.

- To introduce pressure, set a target score. If you do not reach it, give yourself one opportunity to hit a drive to within 20 yards of a target, followed by a 7 iron to within 30ft of a target, with a consequence of repeating the practice or choosing an unwelcome penalty.

- Record your scores and next time aim to score more points. Every time you set a new personal best, write it down. Be proud of your progress and celebrate your success!

Scoring System

Club	Inside 10ft	Inside 20ft	Inside 30ft/10yds	Inside 15yds	Inside 20yds
Driver (D)	5	4	3	2	1
Iron (I)	3	2	1	0	0

Shot	1	2	3	4	5	6	7	8	9	10
Club	D	I	D	I	D	I	D	I	D	I
Score										
Too L / R										

Shot	11	12	13	14	15	16	17	18	19	20
Club	D	I	D	I	D	I	D	I	D	I
Score										
Too L / R										

Shot	21	22	23	24	25	26	27	28	Total	
Club	D	I	D	I	D	I	D	I		
Score										
Too L / R									L	R

Driver			Irons		
Score	Too Far Left	Too Far Right	Score	Too Far Left	Too Far Right

Through the Bag

This is a 36-shot practice divided into two 18-shot sets. Choose the most appropriate target for each club and always measure the distance to it. Vary the wedges, short, mid and long irons or hybrids you use, so that you incorporate all of the clubs in your bag.

Equipment: All of your clubs, 36 balls, tees, laser rangefinder, notebook, pen

(Use a launch monitor to receive carry distance and accuracy feedback after every shot if you have access to one).

- Choose a small, precise target for each shot.

- Use targets on the range, objects in the background or your best judgement to determine your accuracy.

- With your driver choose a target and a minimum distance the ball must fly or choose a target the ball must fly over.

- Follow the shot order on the scorecard.

- Go through your pre-shot routine before every shot.

- Use the scoring system to score your accuracy. Fill in the scorecard after every shot.

- Can your second set beat your first set?

- To introduce pressure, set a target score. If you do not reach it, give yourself one opportunity to hit a drive to within 20 yards of a target, followed by a short iron to within 30ft of a different target, with a consequence of repeating the practice or choosing an unwelcome penalty.

- Record your scores and next time aim to score more points. Every time you set a new personal best, write

it down. Be proud of your progress and celebrate your success!

Scoring System					
Club	Inside 10ft	Inside 20ft	Inside 30ft/10yds	Inside 15yds	Inside 20yds
Driver	5	4	3	2	1
Fwy / Hybrid	4	3	2	1	0
Iron	3	2	1	0	0
Wedge	2	1	0	0	0

Dr Nicky Lumb & Dr Dave Alred MBE

Set 1

Shot	1	2	3	4	5	6	7	8	9	Total
Club	D	W	LI or HY	SI	D	MI	SI	FW	W	
Distance										
Score										

Shot	10	11	12	13	14	15	16	17	18	Total
Club	LI or HY	D	W	SI	MI	W	MI	D	SI	
Distance										
Score										

Key: D = Driver, FW = Fairway Wood, HY = Hybrid, LI = Long Iron, MI = Mid Iron, SI = Short Iron, W = Wedge	Final Total:	

Set 2

Shot	1	2	3	4	5	6	7	8	9	Total
Club	D	LI or HY	W	SI	D	MI	W	SI	MI	
Distance										
Score										

Shot	10	11	12	13	14	15	16	17	18	Total
Club	SI	D	W	FW	LI	W	MI	D	SI	
Distance										
Score										

	Final Total:	

Odd vs. Even

This is a 36-shot practice that involves hitting drives and approach shots between 50 and 180 yards.

The first set of 18 shots consists of hitting balls to odd numbered distances and the second set to even numbered distances.

Can you beat your odd numbered score with the even numbered distances on the second set?

This practice is easier to complete with a launch monitor or device which gives distance feedback and accuracy after each shot. If you don't have access to one, you will still benefit greatly by using your best judgement.

Equipment: All of your clubs, 36 balls, tees, laser rangefinder, notebook, pen

- Choose a small, precise target for each shot.

- Use targets on the range, objects in the background or your best judgement to determine your accuracy.

- With your driver choose a target and a minimum distance the ball must fly or choose a target the ball must fly over.

- Follow the shot order on the scorecard.

- Go through your pre-shot routine before every shot.

- Use the scoring system to score your accuracy. Fill in the scorecard after every shot.

Dr Nicky Lumb & Dr Dave Alred MBE

- To introduce pressure, set a target score. If you do not reach it, give yourself one opportunity to hit a drive to within 20 yards of a target followed by a shot from 125 yards to within 30ft of a target, with a consequence of repeating the practice or choosing an unwelcome penalty.

- Record your scores and next time aim to score more points. Every time you set a new personal best, write it down. Be proud of your progress and celebrate your success!

Scoring System

Club	Inside 10ft	Inside 20ft	Inside 30ft/10yds	Inside 15yds	Inside 20yds
Driver	5	4	3	2	1
Fwy/Hybrid	4	3	2	1	0
Iron	3	2	1	0	0
Wedge	2	1	0	0	0

Set 1 - Odd Numbers

Shot	1	2	3	4	5	6	7	8	9	Total
Club	D	55 yds	175 yds	105 yds	D	155 yds	75 yds	145 yds	85 yds	
Score										

Shot	10	11	12	13	14	15	16	17	18	Total
Club	175 yds	D	65 yds	115 yds	165 yds	95 yds	135 yds	D	125 yds	
Score										

Key: D = Driver   Final Total: | |

Set 2 - Even Numbers

Shot	1	2	3	4	5	6	7	8	9	Total
Club	D	50 yds	180 yds	100 yds	D	150 yds	70 yds	140 yds	80 yds	
Score										

Shot	10	11	12	13	14	15	16	17	18	Total
Club	170 yds	D	60 yds	110 yds	160 yds	90 yds	130 yds	D	120 yds	
Score										

Final Score: | |

   Dr Nicky Lumb & Dr Dave Alred MBE

Play a Course on the Range

Equipment: All of your clubs, balls, tees, notebook, pen

Imagine you are playing a golf course on the driving range. Choose a course; you can even print a scorecard off the internet.

Envisage the first hole is a straight 380-yard par 4. Choose a fairway area, and hit your drive. If the ball finishes within your designated fairway, hit a short iron or wedge to a certain distance as if it was your approach shot into the green. If your drive missed the fairway, use the club you would need if your ball was in light rough. If your drive was wayward, you may need a wedge to get the ball back onto the fairway.

By imagining you are playing a round of golf, the result of one shot determines the next. This creates the element of unpredictability you face on the course. While you are doing this, go through and score your full pre-shot routine on every shot.

Keep your supply of balls away from the hitting area so you have to collect your next ball between shots. If there is a putting and chipping green close by, use it to play these shots within your round. If there isn't, do your best to improvise. Driving range carpets have been known to act as great putting greens!

Hole	Drive — Fairway Club	Tee Shot — Process Pre	Tee Shot — Process Post	Approach — Green Approach	Approach — Club/Dist.	Approach — Process Pre	Approach — Process Post	Chip — Club/Dist.	Chip — Process Pre	Chip — Process Post	Putts — Dist(s).	Putts — No.	Putts — Process Pre	Putts — Process Post	Score	Par
1	<< < O > >> / v ∧			<< < O > >> / v ∧												
2	<< < O > >> / v ∧			<< < O > >> / v ∧												
3	<< < O > >> / v ∧			<< < O > >> / v ∧												
4	<< < O > >> / v ∧			<< < O > >> / v ∧												
5	<< < O > >> / v ∧			<< < O > >> / v ∧												
6	<< < O > >> / v ∧			<< < O > >> / v ∧												
7	<< < O > >> / v ∧			<< < O > >> / v ∧												
8	<< < O > >> / v ∧			<< < O > >> / v ∧												
9	<< < O > >> / v ∧			<< < O > >> / v ∧												
10	<< < O > >> / v ∧			<< < O > >> / v ∧												
11	<< < O > >> / v ∧			<< < O > >> / v ∧												
12	<< < O > >> / v ∧			<< < O > >> / v ∧												
13	<< < O > >> / v ∧			<< < O > >> / v ∧												
14	<< < O > >> / v ∧			<< < O > >> / v ∧												
15	<< < O > >> / v ∧			<< < O > >> / v ∧												
16	<< < O > >> / v ∧			<< < O > >> / v ∧												
17	<< < O > >> / v ∧			<< < O > >> / v ∧												
18	<< < O > >> / v ∧			<< < O > >> / v ∧												
Total																

<< Left of fwy/green in trouble   < Left of fwy/green   O Hit fwy/green   > Right of fwy/green   >> Right of fwy/green in trouble   v Short   ∧ Long

Dist(s) - Putt distances. No. Number of putts. Process - Your pre-shot and/or post-shot process scores on each shot out of 10.

Dr Nicky Lumb & Dr Dave Alred MBE

ON THE COURSE

Within this section there are a number of multi-ball practices. If a course is busy, adapt any practice by using less balls or alternate the holes you apply the practice on so that you don't delay play!

With every practice, always hole out. You have to do this in every stroke-play competition, so it's best to do it in practice as well.

THROUGH THE BAG

Multi-Ball Practices

3 Balls Best Ball

3 Balls Best Ball shows you what you can achieve with your current skills. It involves hitting 3 shots from every position, choosing the best ball every time and then playing 3 shots from there.

(If a course is busy, you can do this practice with 2 balls. Please don't delay play!)

- Number 3 balls: 1, 2 and 3.

- Stand on the tee, choose your strategy and visualise how you intend to play the hole shot by shot.

- Hit each ball. On every shot, choose a small, precise target and go through your pre-shot routine.

- Choose the best ball, circle its number on the scorecard and play your next 3 shots from there.

- If a shot does not match your intention, work out how you can make the next one better so you get maximum benefit from every extra ball.

- Play 9 or 18 holes.

- How low you can go?

- How many times did you use ball 1, 2 or 3?

- Record your scores and next time aim to score one shot better. Every time you set a new personal best, write it down. Be proud of your progress and celebrate your success!

Dr Nicky Lumb & Dr Dave Alred MBE

Hole	Par	Score	*	1	2	3	4	5	6	7	8
1				1 2 3	1 2 3	1 2 3	1 2 3	1 2 3	1 2 3	1 2 3	1 2 3
2				1 2 3	1 2 3	1 2 3	1 2 3	1 2 3	1 2 3	1 2 3	1 2 3
3				1 2 3	1 2 3	1 2 3	1 2 3	1 2 3	1 2 3	1 2 3	1 2 3
4				1 2 3	1 2 3	1 2 3	1 2 3	1 2 3	1 2 3	1 2 3	1 2 3
5				1 2 3	1 2 3	1 2 3	1 2 3	1 2 3	1 2 3	1 2 3	1 2 3
6				1 2 3	1 2 3	1 2 3	1 2 3	1 2 3	1 2 3	1 2 3	1 2 3
7				1 2 3	1 2 3	1 2 3	1 2 3	1 2 3	1 2 3	1 2 3	1 2 3
8				1 2 3	1 2 3	1 2 3	1 2 3	1 2 3	1 2 3	1 2 3	1 2 3
9				1 2 3	1 2 3	1 2 3	1 2 3	1 2 3	1 2 3	1 2 3	1 2 3
Total				1 2 3	1 2 3	1 2 3	1 2 3	1 2 3	1 2 3	1 2 3	1 2 3

Hole	Par	Score	*	1	2	3	4	5	6	7	8
10				1 2 3	1 2 3	1 2 3	1 2 3	1 2 3	1 2 3	1 2 3	1 2 3
11				1 2 3	1 2 3	1 2 3	1 2 3	1 2 3	1 2 3	1 2 3	1 2 3
12				1 2 3	1 2 3	1 2 3	1 2 3	1 2 3	1 2 3	1 2 3	1 2 3
13				1 2 3	1 2 3	1 2 3	1 2 3	1 2 3	1 2 3	1 2 3	1 2 3
14				1 2 3	1 2 3	1 2 3	1 2 3	1 2 3	1 2 3	1 2 3	1 2 3
15				1 2 3	1 2 3	1 2 3	1 2 3	1 2 3	1 2 3	1 2 3	1 2 3
16				1 2 3	1 2 3	1 2 3	1 2 3	1 2 3	1 2 3	1 2 3	1 2 3
17				1 2 3	1 2 3	1 2 3	1 2 3	1 2 3	1 2 3	1 2 3	1 2 3
18				1 2 3	1 2 3	1 2 3	1 2 3	1 2 3	1 2 3	1 2 3	1 2 3
Total				1 2 3	1 2 3	1 2 3	1 2 3	1 2 3	1 2 3	1 2 3	1 2 3

* Use to score one of your processes within your pre-shot or post-shot routine

One Ball Nine Bonus Shots

Play one ball with the option of up to nine second chance shots. If you decide to hit the second ball, you have to play on from wherever it finishes, so this practice introduces pressure.

- Number 2 balls: 1 and 2.
- Stand on the tee, choose your strategy and visualise how you intend to play the hole shot by shot.
- On every shot, choose a small, precise target and go through your pre-shot routine.
- If a shot does not match your intention, you have the option of playing ball 2, but once you put that ball into play, you have to continue playing the hole with it.
- Play 9 or 18 holes.
- You have the option of using ball 2 on up to 9 shots.
- When you use ball 2, circle it on the scorecard.
- How low you can go?
- How many times did you use ball 2?
- Record your scores and next time aim to score one shot better. Every time you set a new personal best, write it down. Be proud of your progress and celebrate your success!

Dr Nicky Lumb & Dr Dave Alred MBE

Hole	Par	Score	*	1	2	3	4	5	6	7	8
1				1 2	1 2	1 2	1 2	1 2	1 2	1 2	1 2
2				1 2	1 2	1 2	1 2	1 2	1 2	1 2	1 2
3				1 2	1 2	1 2	1 2	1 2	1 2	1 2	1 2
4				1 2	1 2	1 2	1 2	1 2	1 2	1 2	1 2
5				1 2	1 2	1 2	1 2	1 2	1 2	1 2	1 2
6				1 2	1 2	1 2	1 2	1 2	1 2	1 2	1 2
7				1 2	1 2	1 2	1 2	1 2	1 2	1 2	1 2
8				1 2	1 2	1 2	1 2	1 2	1 2	1 2	1 2
9				1 2	1 2	1 2	1 2	1 2	1 2	1 2	1 2
Total				1 2	1 2	1 2	1 2	1 2	1 2	1 2	1 2
Hole	Par	Score	*	1	2	3	4	5	6	7	8
10				1 2	1 2	1 2	1 2	1 2	1 2	1 2	1 2
11				1 2	1 2	1 2	1 2	1 2	1 2	1 2	1 2
12				1 2	1 2	1 2	1 2	1 2	1 2	1 2	1 2
13				1 2	1 2	1 2	1 2	1 2	1 2	1 2	1 2
14				1 2	1 2	1 2	1 2	1 2	1 2	1 2	1 2
15				1 2	1 2	1 2	1 2	1 2	1 2	1 2	1 2
16				1 2	1 2	1 2	1 2	1 2	1 2	1 2	1 2
17				1 2	1 2	1 2	1 2	1 2	1 2	1 2	1 2
18				1 2	1 2	1 2	1 2	1 2	1 2	1 2	1 2
Total				1 2	1 2	1 2	1 2	1 2	1 2	1 2	1 2

* Use to score one of your processes within your pre-shot or post-shot routine

3 Balls Worst Ball

3 Ball Worst Ball creates pressure and tests your consistency and patience. It is tough!

(If a course is busy, you can do this practice with 2 balls. Please don't delay play!)

- Number three balls: 1, 2 and 3.

- Stand on the first tee and visualise how you want to play the hole shot by shot.

- Hit each ball. On every shot, choose a small, precise target, set a clear intention and go through your pre-shot routine.

- Choose the worst ball, circle its number on the scorecard and play your next 3 shots from there.

- Repeat this process on every shot for 9 or 18 holes.

- If a shot does not match your intention, work out how you can make the next one better so you get maximum benefit from every extra ball.

- At the end, add up your scores.

- How many times did you use ball 1, 2 or 3?

- Record your scores and next time aim to score one shot better. Every time you set a new personal best, write it down. Be proud of your progress and celebrate your success!

Dr Nicky Lumb & Dr Dave Alred MBE

Hole	Par	Score	*	1	2	3	4	5	6	7	8
1				1 2 3	1 2 3	1 2 3	1 2 3	1 2 3	1 2 3	1 2 3	1 2 3
2				1 2 3	1 2 3	1 2 3	1 2 3	1 2 3	1 2 3	1 2 3	1 2 3
3				1 2 3	1 2 3	1 2 3	1 2 3	1 2 3	1 2 3	1 2 3	1 2 3
4				1 2 3	1 2 3	1 2 3	1 2 3	1 2 3	1 2 3	1 2 3	1 2 3
5				1 2 3	1 2 3	1 2 3	1 2 3	1 2 3	1 2 3	1 2 3	1 2 3
6				1 2 3	1 2 3	1 2 3	1 2 3	1 2 3	1 2 3	1 2 3	1 2 3
7				1 2 3	1 2 3	1 2 3	1 2 3	1 2 3	1 2 3	1 2 3	1 2 3
8				1 2 3	1 2 3	1 2 3	1 2 3	1 2 3	1 2 3	1 2 3	1 2 3
9				1 2 3	1 2 3	1 2 3	1 2 3	1 2 3	1 2 3	1 2 3	1 2 3
Total				1 2 3	1 2 3	1 2 3	1 2 3	1 2 3	1 2 3	1 2 3	1 2 3

Hole	Par	Score	*	1	2	3	4	5	6	7	8
10				1 2 3	1 2 3	1 2 3	1 2 3	1 2 3	1 2 3	1 2 3	1 2 3
11				1 2 3	1 2 3	1 2 3	1 2 3	1 2 3	1 2 3	1 2 3	1 2 3
12				1 2 3	1 2 3	1 2 3	1 2 3	1 2 3	1 2 3	1 2 3	1 2 3
13				1 2 3	1 2 3	1 2 3	1 2 3	1 2 3	1 2 3	1 2 3	1 2 3
14				1 2 3	1 2 3	1 2 3	1 2 3	1 2 3	1 2 3	1 2 3	1 2 3
15				1 2 3	1 2 3	1 2 3	1 2 3	1 2 3	1 2 3	1 2 3	1 2 3
16				1 2 3	1 2 3	1 2 3	1 2 3	1 2 3	1 2 3	1 2 3	1 2 3
17				1 2 3	1 2 3	1 2 3	1 2 3	1 2 3	1 2 3	1 2 3	1 2 3
18				1 2 3	1 2 3	1 2 3	1 2 3	1 2 3	1 2 3	1 2 3	1 2 3
Total				1 2 3	1 2 3	1 2 3	1 2 3	1 2 3	1 2 3	1 2 3	1 2 3

* Use to score one of your processes within your pre-shot or post-shot routine

One Ball Practices

Aim for the Middle

On the course, aiming for the middle of the green is often the smartest and safest option. Low scores are usually achieved by dropping less shots not by making more birdies. This practice will develop your course management skills and improve your ability to play to your own targets so that you stay away from trouble and avoid dangerous flag positions.

- Play 9 or 18 holes.
- Choose a small, precise target in the middle of every green.
- Set a clear intention and go through your pre-shot routine before every shot.
- Tick the box every time you match your intention and hit the ball in the middle of each green.
- Record your score for each hole.
- Record how many shots finish in the middle of the green and your total score. Next time aim to improve each score. Every time you set a new personal best, write it down. Be proud of your progress and celebrate your success!

Dr Nicky Lumb & Dr Dave Alred MBE

Shot	1	2	3	4	5	6	7	8	9	Total
Middle Green										
Score										

Shot	10	11	12	13	14	15	16	17	18	Total
Middle Green										
Score										

	Final Score:	

Aim Left or Right

On the course, there will be times when it will be beneficial for your ball to finish on the left or right side of a fairway or green. Low scores are usually achieved by dropping less shots not by making more birdies. This practice will develop your course management skills and improve your ability to play to your own targets, so that you aim for the safest places, stay away from trouble and avoid dangerous flag positions.

If you like to shape the ball from left to right and right to left, hit every shot that must finish right with a fade and every shot that must finish left with a draw.

- Play 9 or 18 holes
- On every shot choose if you want the ball to finish on the left or right side of the fairway or green.
- Choose a small precise target that accommodates your decision.
- Go through your pre-shot routine before every shot.
- After every shot mark the scorecard with a tick or cross depending on whether your shot finished on the intended side of the fairway or green.
- Record your score for each hole.
- Record your total score and next time aim to hit one more shot that matches your intention and finishes on the correct side of each fairway and green. Every time you set a new personal best, write it down. Be proud of your progress and celebrate your success!

Dr Nicky Lumb & Dr Dave Alred MBE

Shot	1	2	3	4	5	6	7	8	9	Total
Left Fairway										
Right Fairway										
Left Green										
Right Green										
Score										

Shot	10	11	12	13	14	15	16	17	18	Total
Left Fairway										
Right Fairway										
Left Green										
Right Green										
Score										
							Final Score:			

Be Creative with 5 Clubs

On the course, most shot distances will be between clubs, and you will have to decide whether to hit for example a hard 8 iron or an easy 7 iron. Playing with 5 clubs forces you to be creative and imaginative in creating shots and controlling your ball flight and distances. It's great fun too!

- Play 9 or 18 holes using 5 clubs.

- Choose a small, precise target, set a clear intention and go through your pre-shot routine before every shot.

- Record your score for each hole.

- Record your total score and next time aim to be one shot better. Every time you set a new personal best, write it down. Be proud of your progress and celebrate your success!

Clubs:	1		2		3		4		5	
Hole	1	2	3	4	5	6	7	8	9	Total
Score										
Hole	10	11	12	13	14	15	16	17	18	Total
Score										

Final Score:

SPECIFIC SHOT PRACTICES

Putting

Short Putts with an Extra Ball

- On every hole, have one putt from the distances on the scorecard.

- Fill in the scorecard.

- To introduce pressure, set a target score. If you do not reach it, give yourself one opportunity to hole a 5ft putt, with a consequence of repeating the practice on the putting green or choosing an unwelcome penalty.

- Record your total score and next time aim to be one shot better. Every time you set a new personal best, write it down. Be proud of your progress and celebrate your success!

Hole	1	2	3	4	5	6	7	8	9	Total
Distance	3ft	5ft	7ft	9ft	4ft	8ft	6ft	10ft	4ft	
Score										
Hole	10	11	12	13	14	15	16	17	18	Total
Distance	9ft	5ft	3ft	10ft	4ft	6ft	8ft	7ft	4ft	
Score										

Final Score:

Putting with an Extra Ball

- On every hole, putt a ball to completion from the distances on the scorecard.

- Score the following points: 1 putt = -1, 2 putts = 0, 3 putts = +1, 4 putts = +2.

- Fill in the scorecard.

- To introduce pressure, set a target score. If you do not reach it, give yourself one opportunity to two-putt from 30ft, with a consequence of repeating the practice on the putting green or choosing an unwelcome penalty.

- Record your total score and next time aim to be one shot better. Every time you set a new personal best, write it down. Be proud of your progress and celebrate your success!

Hole	1	2	3	4	5	6	7	8	9	Total
Distance	20ft	30ft	40ft	10ft	25ft	15ft	30ft	20ft	35ft	
Score										

Hole	10	11	12	13	14	15	16	17	18	Total
Distance	10ft	25ft	40ft	20ft	30ft	15ft	20ft	35ft	20ft	
Score										

		Final Score:	

Dr Nicky Lumb & Dr Dave Alred MBE

Short Game

Chipping with an Extra Ball

- On every hole, play one ball to completion from any distance between 10 and 20 yards from the hole.

- Each hole is a par 2.

- Throw each ball to a random spot and play it as it lies.

- Include different slopes and lies.

- Always choose a small, precise landing spot, and picture how you want the ball to reach the hole.

- Before every shot, go through your pre-shot routine.

- Always hole out.

- Score the following points: 1 shot = -1, 2 shots = 0, 3 shots = +1, 4 shots = +2.

- To introduce pressure, set a target score. If you do not reach it, give yourself one opportunity to get up and down from 15 yards, with a consequence of choosing an unwelcome penalty.

- Record your total score and next time aim to complete the practice in one shot less. Every time you set a new personal best, write it down. Be proud of your progress and celebrate your success!

Hole	1	2	3	4	5	6	7	8	9	Total
Score										

Hole	10	11	12	13	14	15	16	17	18	Total
Score										

	Final Score:	

Chipping Accuracy Challenge

- On each hole, play one ball from two different positions between 10 and 20 yards from the hole.

- Score 2 points for every shot that finishes inside 3ft and 1 point for every shot that finishes inside 6ft?

- To introduce pressure, set a target score. If you do not reach it, give yourself one opportunity to get up and down from 20 yards, with a consequence of repeating the practice on the chipping green or choosing an unwelcome penalty.

- Record your total score and next time aim to get an extra shot inside each scoring zone. Every time you set a new personal best, write it down. Be proud of your progress and celebrate your success!

Hole	1	2	3	4	5	6	7	8	9	Total
Score										

Hole	10	11	12	13	14	15	16	17	18	Total
Score										

		Final Score:	

Dr Nicky Lumb & Dr Dave Alred MBE

Approach Shots to the Green - Pitching

Pitching with an Extra Ball

- On every hole, play a ball to completion from the distances on the scorecard.

- Every hole is a par 3.

- Fill in the scorecard.

- To introduce pressure, set a target score. If you do not reach it, give yourself one opportunity to hole out in three shots or less from 90 yards, with a consequence of choosing an unwelcome penalty.

- Record your total score and next time aim to be one shot better. Every time you set a new personal best, write it down. Be proud of your progress and celebrate your success!

Hole	1	2	3	4	5	6	7	8	9	Total
Dist. (yds)	50	60	70	80	90	100	50	60	70	
Score										

Hole	10	11	12	13	14	15	16	17	18	Total
Dist. (yds)	80	90	100	50	60	70	80	90	100	
Score										

Final Score:

Pitching Accuracy Challenge

(If a course is busy, you can do this practice with 1 or 2 balls. Please don't delay play!)

- On each hole, play 3 balls into the green from the stated yardage.

- Score 3 points for every shot that finishes inside 6ft, 2 points for every shot that finishes inside 10ft and 1 point for every shot that finishes inside 20ft.

- To introduce pressure, set a target score. If you do not reach it, give yourself one opportunity to hole out in three shots or less from 100 yards, with a consequence of choosing an unwelcome penalty.

- Record your score and next time aim to get an extra shot inside each scoring zone. Every time you set a new personal best, write it down. Be proud of your progress and celebrate your success!

Hole	1	2	3	4	5	6	7	8	9	Total
Dist. (yds)	50	60	70	80	90	100	50	60	70	
Score										

Hole	10	11	12	13	14	15	16	17	18	Total
Dist. (yds)	80	90	100	50	60	70	80	90	100	
Score										

Final Score:

Dr Nicky Lumb & Dr Dave Alred MBE

Approach Shots to the Green - Irons

Iron Accuracy Challenge

(If a course is busy, you can do this practice with 1 or 2 balls. Please don't delay play!)

- On each hole, play 3 balls into the green from the stated yardage.

- Score 3 points for every shot that finishes inside 10ft, 2 points for every shot that finishes inside 20ft and 1 point for every shot that finishes inside 30ft.

- To introduce pressure, set a target score. If you do not reach it, give yourself one opportunity to hole out in three shots or less from 120 yards, with a consequence of choosing an unwelcome penalty.

- Record your score and next time aim to get an extra shot inside each scoring zone. Every time you set a new personal best, write it down. Be proud of your progress and celebrate your success!

- As your skills progress, adapt this practice so that it includes the one or two yardage bands you play from the most on the course.

Hole	1	2	3	4	5	6	7	8	9	Total
Dist. (yds)	100	110	120	130	140	150	100	110	120	
Score										

Hole	10	11	12	13	14	15	16	17	18	Total
Dist. (yds)	130	140	150	100	110	120	130	140	150	
Score										

	Final Score:	

Playing to the Front and Back of a Green

On the course, there will be times when it is beneficial for your ball to finish on the front half or back half of a green. This practice will prepare you for these situations.

- On each hole, play 2 balls into the green from the stated yardage. Play one ball to finish on the front half of the green and the other to finish on the back half.

- How many shots finish in the intended half?

- To introduce pressure, set a target score. If you do not reach it, give yourself one opportunity to hole out in three shots or less from 120 yards, with a consequence of choosing an unwelcome penalty.

- Record your score and next time aim to get an extra shot in the desired half. Every time you set a new personal best, write it down. Be proud of your progress and celebrate your success!

- As your skills progress, adapt this practice so that it includes the one or two yardage bands you play from the most on the course.

Hole	1	2	3	4	5	6	7	8	9	Total
Dist. (yds)	100	110	120	130	140	150	100	110	120	
Front										
Back										

Hole	10	11	12	13	14	15	16	17	18	Total
Dist. (yds)	130	140	150	100	110	120	130	140	150	
Front										
Back										

Dr Nicky Lumb & Dr Dave Alred MBE

Playing to the Left and Right of a Green

On the course, there will be times when it is beneficial for your ball to finish on one side of the green so you can attack a pin or avoid trouble. This practice will prepare you for these situations and get you used to selecting and aiming at your own targets instead of the flag.

- On each hole, play 2 balls into the green from the stated yardage. Play one ball to the left side of the green and the other to the right side.

- How many shots finish on the intended side of the green?

- If you like to shape the ball, hit the shots to the left side of the green with a draw from right to left, and hit shots to the right side of the green with a fade from left or right.

- To introduce pressure, set a target score. If you do not reach it, give yourself one opportunity to hit a shot to your chosen side of the green from 120 yards and to hole out in three shots or less, with a consequence of choosing an unwelcome penalty.

- Record your score and next time aim to get an extra shot in the desired half. Every time you set a new personal best, write it down. Be proud of your progress and celebrate your success!

- As your skills progress, adapt this practice so that it includes the one or two yardage bands you play from the most on the course.

Hole	1	2	3	4	5	6	7	8	9	Total
Dist. (yds)	100	110	120	130	140	150	100	110	120	
Left										
Right										

Hole	10	11	12	13	14	15	16	17	18	Total
Dist. (yds)	130	140	150	100	110	120	130	140	150	
Left										
Right										

Dr Nicky Lumb & Dr Dave Alred MBE

Off the Tee

3 Drives Best Ball

(If a course is busy, you can do this practice with 2 balls. Please don't delay play!)

- Number three balls: 1, 2 and 3.

- Hit 3 shots off every tee.

- Choose the best positioned ball and continue playing the hole with that ball.

- Mark on the scorecard which number drive you played the hole with.

- If a drive does not match your intention, work out how you can make the next one better so you get maximum benefit from every extra ball.

- Play 9 or 18 holes.

- Record your score and next time aim to shoot one shot less. Every time you set a new personal best, write it down. Be proud of your progress and celebrate your success!

	1	2	3	4	5	6	7	8	9	Total
Tee Shot	1 2 3	1 2 3	1 2 3	1 2 3	1 2 3	1 2 3	1 2 3	1 2 3	1 2 3	
Score										

	10	11	12	13	14	15	16	17	18	Total
Tee Shot	1 2 3	1 2 3	1 2 3	1 2 3	1 2 3	1 2 3	1 2 3	1 2 3	1 2 3	
Score										

3 Drives Worst Ball

(If a course is busy, you can do this practice with 2 balls. Please don't delay play!)

- Number three balls: 1, 2 and 3.

- Hit 3 shots off every tee.

- Choose the worst positioned ball and continue playing the hole with that ball.

- Mark on the scorecard which number drive you played the hole with.

- If a drive does not match your intention, work out how you can make the next one better so you get maximum benefit from every extra ball.

- Play 9 or 18 holes.

- Record your score and next time aim to shoot one shot less. Every time you set a new personal best, write it down. Be proud of your progress and celebrate your success!

	1	2	3	4	5	6	7	8	9	Total
Tee Shot	1 2 3	1 2 3	1 2 3	1 2 3	1 2 3	1 2 3	1 2 3	1 2 3	1 2 3	
Score										

	10	11	12	13	14	15	16	17	18	Total
Tee Shot	1 2 3	1 2 3	1 2 3	1 2 3	1 2 3	1 2 3	1 2 3	1 2 3	1 2 3	
Score										

Dr Nicky Lumb & Dr Dave Alred MBE

Off the Tee Accuracy

- On every tee, choose a small, precise target.
- Complete your pre-shot routine before every tee shot.
- Hit 3 shots off every tee.
- If a tee shot does not match your intention, work out how you can make the next one better so you get maximum benefit from every extra ball.
- Complete the hole with your first ball.
- Play 9 or 18 holes.
- Fill in the scorecard. Score points for your accuracy using the scoring system.
- To introduce pressure, set a target score. If you do not reach it, chose an unwelcome penalty.
- Record your score and next time aim to score one more point. Every time you set a new personal best, write it down. Be proud of your progress and celebrate your success!

Scoring System

Club	Inside 10ft	Inside 20ft	Inside 30ft/10yds	Inside 15yds	Inside 20yds
Driver	5	4	3	2	1
Fwy / Hybrid	4	3	2	1	0
Iron	3	2	1	0	0

Hole	1	2	3	4	5	6	7	8	9	Total
Tee Shot 1										
Tee Shot 2										
Tee Shot 3										

Hole	10	11	12	13	14	15	16	17	18	Total
Tee Shot 1										
Tee Shot 2										
Tee Shot 3										
								Final Total:		

Dr Nicky Lumb & Dr Dave Alred MBE

COLLECTING YOUR SCORES

The scorecard will help you to collect all of your performance and process scores when you are playing on the course. You can use the results charts to collate and analyse your scores and monitor your performances over time.

Scorecard

	Drive	Tee Shot		Approach				Chip					Putts						
	Fairway	Process		Green Approach	Club /	Process		Club /		Process				Process				Score	Par
	Club	Pre	Post		Dist.	Pre	Post	Dist.	Dist(s).	Pre	Post	No.	Pre	Post					
1	<< < O ^ >> <			<< < O ^ >> < v vv															
2	<< < O ^ >> <			<< < O ^ >> < v vv															
3	<< < O ^ >> <			<< < O ^ >> < v vv															
4	<< < O ^ >> <			<< < O ^ >> < v vv															
5	<< < O ^ >> <			<< < O ^ >> < v vv															
6	<< < O ^ >> <			<< < O ^ >> < v vv															
7	<< < O ^ >> <			<< < O ^ >> < v vv															
8	<< < O ^ >> <			<< < O ^ >> < v vv															
9	<< < O ^ >> <			<< < O ^ >> < v vv															
10	<< < O ^ >> <			<< < O ^ >> < v vv															
11	<< < O ^ >> <			<< < O ^ >> < v vv															
12	<< < O ^ >> <			<< < O ^ >> < v vv															
13	<< < O ^ >> <			<< < O ^ >> < v vv															
14	<< < O ^ >> <			<< < O ^ >> < v vv															
15	<< < O ^ >> <			<< < O ^ >> < v vv															
16	<< < O ^ >> <			<< < O ^ >> < v vv															
17	<< < O ^ >> <			<< < O ^ >> < v vv															
18	<< < O ^ >> <			<< < O ^ >> < v vv															
Total																			

<< Left of fwy/green in trouble   < Left of fwy/green   O Hit fwy/green   > Right of fwy/green   >> Right of fwy/green in trouble   V Short   ∧ Long

Dist(s) - Putt distances. No. Number of putts. Process - Your pre-shot and/or post-shot process scores on each shot out of 10.

Dr Nicky Lumb & Dr Dave Alred MBE

betterpractice
bettergolf.com

Playing Statistics Results Analysis Charts

Tee Shots	<<	<	O	>	>>
Total					

Distances	< 3ft	3-6ft	< 10ft	10-20ft	> 20ft
< 10yds					
10-20yds					
20-30yds					
> 30yds					
Total					

Distances	< 10ft	10-20ft	20-30ft	> 30ft	<	>	<<	>>
50-75yds								
75-100yds								
100-125yds								
125-150yds								
150-175yds								
175-200yds								
200-225yds								
225-250yds								
Total								

Putt Lengths		1st Putt	2nd Putt	3rd Putt
	< 3ft			
	3-5ft			
	6-10ft			
	10-20ft			
	20-30ft			
	> 30ft			
	Total			

Process Score Totals							
Tee Shot		Approach		Chip		Putts	
Pre	Post	Pre	Post	Pre	Post	Pre	Post

Dr Nicky Lumb & Dr Dave Alred MBE

Process Scorecard

			Pre-Shot Process Scorecard								
Hole	Par	Hole Score	Process Score	1	2	3	4	5	6	7	8
1											
2											
3											
4											
5											
6											
7											
8											
9											
Total											
Hole	Par	Hole Score	Process Score	1	2	3	4	5	6	7	8
10											
11											
12											
13											
14											
15											
16											
17											
18											
Total											

Post-Shot Process Scorecard

Post-Shot Process Scorecard											
Hole	Par	Hole Score	Process Score	1	2	3	4	5	6	7	8
1											
2											
3											
4											
5											
6											
7											
8											
9											
Total											
Hole	Par	Hole Score	Process Score	1	2	3	4	5	6	7	8
10											
11											
12											
13											
14											
15											
16											
17											
18											
Total											

Dr Nicky Lumb & Dr Dave Alred MBE

Congratulations on completing

Better Practice Better Golf!

For more information visit

BetterPracticeBetterGolf.com

Other Books in the Better Practice Better Golf series:
Putting Practice Workbook
Short Game Practice Workbook
Long Game Practice Workbook
On the Course Practice Workbook
Pre and Post Shot Routine Practice Workbook
Performance and Playing Statistics Workbook

Printed in Great Britain
by Amazon

22153856R00165